Pacific Northwest

GARDEN SURVIVAL GUIDE

Debra Prinzing

FULCRUM PUBLISHING
Golden, Colorado

To Bruce

Thank you for hauling my compost, digging my holes, and believing in me all these years.

Text copyright © 2004 Debra Prinzing

ISBN 1-55591-502-7
Library of Congress Cataloging-in-Publication Data

Prinzing, Debra.
  The garden survival guide : Pacific Northwest / Debra Prinzing.
      p. cm.
  Includes index.
  ISBN 1-55591-502-7 (pbk.)
  1. Gardening--Northwest, Pacific. I. Title.
  SB453.2.N83P75 2004
  635'.09795--dc22

                                    2004001736

Printed in the United States of America
0 9 8 7 6 5 4 3 2 1

Editorial: Cathy Wilkinson Barash, Faith Marcovecchio, Katie Raymond
Design: Ann W. Douden
Cover image: Mindy Dwyer

FULCRUM PUBLISHING
16100 Table Mountain Parkway, Suite 300
Golden, Colorado 80403
(800) 992-2908 • (303) 277-1623
www.fulcrum-books.com

Contents

CONTENTS

V

*If you're new
to this passionate endeavor
of gardening, welcome.
I wish you a wonderful journey
that will introduce you to many
generous and supportive gardening friends.
If you're a seasoned veteran,
add these ideas to your own
and pass along sage advice
to a beginner.*

*My personal wish for each of you is this:
may your gardens be free of slugs,
may your soil be rich and organic,
and may you enjoy equal parts
of rain and sunshine.*

Debra Prinzing

1

Introduction

I recently bought an 'Alicia Amherst' hebe, a showy shrub with chubby purple-tinged leaves and deep-purple flowers. The plant tag read, "Hardiness may be 15° F—survived '98 winter in containers!" Clearly these words were written by a Northwest grower, someone whose years of experience have taught him that gardening with semihardy hebes is a risky endeavor. But there's something revealing about this plant tag's promise. The winter of 1998 was indeed the last one in recent memory during which I raced around yanking cherished pots of tender perennials indoors during the combination rain-freeze-rain-freeze weather.

I learned something surprising from that experience: many plants believe in reincarnation. Even though I thought my New Zealand flax had bit the dust that winter, shrinking down to mush in its concrete container perched on an elevated pedestal exposed to the elements, I couldn't bring myself to toss it onto the compost heap. Almost without thinking, I stuck its remains in the ground, centering the decimated crown between two Himalayan birches. Today I have a four-foot-tall, healthy clump of wine-colored blades soaring upward toward the branches of those birch trees. The lesson I learned that I pass on to you is that plants are tougher than you think. You just need to give them the right conditions in which to thrive.

Providing the plants you love with ideal growing conditions is an essential theme of the *Pacific Northwest Garden Survival Guide*. If you take a down-to-earth approach to gardening, accepting the prevailing climate trends and geographic realities of this region, you're already halfway toward being a successful gardener. The good news is that there are countless resources at hand for outsmarting the whims and ways of Mother Nature.

Whenever I take a plant identification class, I walk away convinced that each of the plants I want for my garden requires "moist, well-drained soil." That little notation in the margins of my notebook, MWDS, once worried me. I knew my rocky clay soil was moist—no doubt about it. But there was no way it could be described as well drained. How could I ever have a beautiful, lush, healthy garden in my pebble-filled 7,200-square-foot patch of earth?

Thankfully, time, experience, and the wisdom of many gardening friends have taught me how to work with the very conditions I once feared. Gardening from the ground up may not be sexy, but it is a proven approach that ensures you won't be frustrated with perennials that sizzle by mid-July or shrubs that drown in standing water during February rains.

The *Pacific Northwest Garden Survival Guide* will equip you with the background and tools you'll need to adjust to the new reality facing our region. Our wet winters are warming ever so slightly, allowing the semihardy hebe and New Zealand flax to usually make it through the season intact. Our dry summers are getting drier. During 2002 Seattle received less than five inches of precipitation from May 1 through November 1. It seems that May and October are the only "normal" months left during which we enjoy a reasonable balance of wet and dry days.

Added to these extremes are the subtle side effects of climate and weather changes. Weeds, pests, and diseases seem to love these new conditions much more than beneficial insects and ornamental plants do. Which brings us to these questions: Is it possible to eradicate unwanted garden visitors without using toxic treatments? Can you learn to tolerate a certain amount of nibbled foliage or the troublesome oxalis between the cracks? The solution is to strike a posture of moderation. A healthy appreciation for that which you can control and an acceptance of that which is out of your control is a good starting point. Small changes in attitudes and practices will go a long way toward responsibly treating our precious environment and the natural beauty of the Northwest.

Our gardens may have fences, but they're not isolated—they're interrelated. Consider the consequences each time a zealous neighbor sprays Roundup on English ivy (a futile endeavor anyway), especially on a windy day. Living above Lake Washington, I'm extremely aware that the products I spray, spread, or pour on my plants on Fifty-second Avenue South will flow downhill and pollute the beautiful lake below that I admire so much each day.

If you're passionate about our amazing corner of the country, if you want to enjoy time in the garden instead of viewing the landscape as a burden or a duty, if you are ready to embrace the growing conditions (good and bad) and work with them, this is the book for you.

This survival guide is a handy reference containing easy-to-read information, ideas, and inspiration for cultivating a Northwest garden in a changing environment. Each regional concern is addressed with a measure of reality and pragmatism. The accessible format features quick tips that will help you solve gardening problems, tackle design challenges, and choose plants that will flourish in your landscape. The book also includes insightful interviews with notable Northwest garden experts whose observations and wisdom offer new perspectives on our region's landscape.

The guide emerged from ideas for solving a set of problems; namely, how you and other Northwest gardeners can adapt and adjust your practices in response to the ecological and geographical challenges of today. When you understand the environment in which you garden, you appreciate the climate in which you live; when you cherish the ground in which you dig, you can work with rather than fight against nature.

This book is divided into three major sections: "Geography," "Wild Weather and Changing Climates," and "Invaders."

"Geography" offers a snapshot of our region's many environments, with particular attention to analyzing your own backyard and understanding its unique zones, soil conditions, and microclimates.

"Wild Weather and Changing Climates" takes a look at the two extremes faced by Northwest gardeners—too much water and too little water—and how to sensibly cope with them in the context of a residential garden.

"Invaders" surveys everything from invasive weeds to pests of every size—and how to organically coexist with some and discourage others that settle in your garden.

You also will find useful appendices at the end of the book, with suggestions of great Pacific Northwest resources, gardening organizations, nurseries, and Web sites.

5

GEOGRAPHY

KNOWING the PLACE

We are intrinsically linked to the soil in which we grow our beloved plants. The backyard we lovingly tend doesn't exist in a vacuum: our landscape draws its character from our surroundings, be they urban, suburban, or rural. When we begin to understand the character of our region's trees, rocks, dirt, topography, temperature, and seasons, we begin to know our place on Earth. Here's where our skills of observation are most keenly put to use; to succeed as a gardener, we need to continually pay attention—to watch, listen, touch, and experience our environment. Practice the fine art of "hanging around" in your own backyard! The more you appreciate and recognize the unique profile of how "place" defines your garden, the more comfortable and successful you'll be.

What's in a Zone?

Like disclosing the zodiac sign under which you were born, identifying your "zonal sign" can provide you with considerable identity—though in this case horticultural rather than temperamental. It is important to know that the United States Department of Agriculture (USDA) Hardiness Zones are based on the average *minimum* cold temperatures. In Seattle's Seward Park neighborhood, located just two blocks uphill from mild-mannered Lake Washington, my garden exists somewhere between USDA Hardiness Zone 8a (10° to

15° F) and 8b (15° to 20° F). The Hardiness Zone listed on a plant tag or in a book indicates which perennials, shrubs, trees, and vines will winter over in the garden and survive for many years. Knowing a plant's hardiness (you don't have to memorize it, there are plenty of references) is important for a number of good reasons, not the least of which is saving yourself the frustration of killing off tender specimens because they just can't cope with your region's backyard conditions.

American gardeners have used the USDA Plant Hardiness Zone Map for more than four decades, and it is the standard guide to which most gardeners turn. When you purchase a plant at the garden center, the number printed on the tag refers to lowest USDA Hardiness Zone in which it will grow.

The USDA's map is currently under review and being updated (although not yet formally released) by the agency's Agricultural Research Service. The map was last updated in 1990; the advent of a new one will help us interpret whether we're experiencing global warming, or as Anne Raver in a *New York Times* article called it, "global weirding."

In compiling the new map, the USDA has taken into consideration more than a decade of weather patterns and other data from 7,000 weather stations nationwide. Temperature highs and lows have changed so dramatically that there are now fifteen zones (four more than on the 1990 map), each of which represents a difference of 10° F in average annual minimum temperatures (Zone 1 represents the coldest winter temperatures; Zone 15 the warmest). The expansion to fifteen zones includes hardiness zones for subtropical and tropical plants.

To see where you are, go to www.usna.usda.gov/ Hardzone/ushzmap.html and explore the North American map. Click on your area of the country. Note the color of your region, and then check the key for temperature highs and lows. Plants suggested in this book include their USDA Zone to help you in choosing the right plants for your region.

What's Your Map Zone?

Once you determine your gardening zone, you have to decide how much it means to you in the grand scheme of things. You may prefer to maintain a cavalier attitude, planting according to the whims of the season. Short-term gratification isn't all bad. However, there's something truly satisfying about choosing the right plant for the right place in your landscape. That has become harder with changing global temperatures and potentially changing USDA Zones. Will your USDA Zone change? The answer is *maybe* and if so, probably *not much*. According to the American Horticultural Society (AHS) (with the help of the Department of Agriculture), information for the update of the current 1990 zone map comes from temperature figures collected between the winter of 1986 and March 2002. During this period, warming temperatures occurred in many areas of the United States. In describing this phenomenon on its Web site, AHS coins it "zone creep," with zones edging slightly northward. The zone ratings don't exist in a vacuum, but offer you a useful tool in plant selection. But other elements are useful as well: compatible soil type with appropriate pH, adequate water, proper exposure to sun or shade, and nutrients are some of those variables that you *can* control. Once you have purchased plants suitable for your garden's temperature range, it's your job to help them thrive once they are out of the nursery pot and in your garden.

▲ ▼ ▲ ▲ ▼ ▼ ▲ ▼ ▲ ▼ ▲ ▼ ▲ ▼ ▲ ▼

OTHER GARDEN RATING SYSTEMS

In addition to the USDA Hardiness Zone map, there are other garden rating systems to guide you, although each uses a different way to measure environmental conditions in the landscape.

Sunset's Climate Zone Map

This map incorporates twenty-four categories in eleven contiguous states (plus Alaska, Hawaii, and southwestern Canada), a rating system that incorporates latitude, ocean/continental air influences, land formations, elevation, water availability, length of growing season, seasonal variations in sun and clouds, rainfall, thermal belts, and other specific regional variables. A look at the 2001 edition of *Sunset's Western Garden Book* puts my garden in their Climate Zone 5, where mild ocean air moderates our winter weather (January minimum temperatures range from 33° to 37° F, with annual lows in the 20s and extremes from 10° to 17° F). To determine your Sunset zone, go to www.sunset.com on the Internet, click on "Garden," and follow the link to "Climate Zones." Here you'll find a map and brief description of this regionalized system to help you evaluate your climate. One of the practical advantages of the Sunset system is the readability of its maps. Each individual Climate Zone map is blown up to a much greater size, permitting far greater detail than the USDA's maps. Having a copy of *Sunset's Western Garden Book,* which includes fabulous plant descriptions and zone-specific plant lists, is also a useful reference for any Northwest gardener.

American Horticultural Society Plant-Heat Zones

This map breaks up the country into twelve regions according to the average number of days above 86° F. The ratings assume that adequate water is supplied to the roots of the plant at all times, because heat damage is linked to insufficient levels of water being available to the plant. To find your heat zone, visit www.ahs.org on the Web, click on "Publications," and select "Heat Zone Map." I typed in my zip code to learn that my neighborhood is somewhere between Zone 2 (one to seven days over 86° F annually) and Zone 3 (seven to fourteen days over 86° F annually). Given the weather that has hit Oregon and Washington gardens in recent summers, one could argue that the Northwest can easily exceed two weeks of 86° F-plus temperatures.

It's interesting and quite useful to see where your own garden falls into these systems. Once you have compared your locale to each chart, you will have an additional level of awareness as well as a reality check when you go plant shopping (especially when looking at the beautiful color pictures in nursery catalogs or on the Internet, where you may be tempted to buy based on appearances alone).

My advice is to be aware of both these benchmarks in addition to the USDA Hardiness Zones. Keep them in mind while designing those windy, sunny, shady, or wet areas of your garden. Remember that there are factors that these ratings systems don't evaluate, such as the amount of sun a plant receives before it is subjected to cold or freezing temperatures; the amount of moisture a plant receives before, during, and after freezing temperatures; and the duration of extreme cold weather.

▲ ▼ ▲ ▲ ▼ ▲ ▼ ▲ ▼ ▲ ▼ ▲ ▼ ▲ ▼

Microclimates

In a recent report, AHS president emeritus Dr. H. Marc Cathey, coordinator of the updated USDA map, stated, "You may have pockets within your garden that are warmer or cooler than the general zone for your area."

His observation offers a concise description of microclimates, the unique areas of your garden that behave differently than you might expect. Many garden microclimates are caused not by nature but by human influence. Your home is indeed the most dominant force in the garden. In one place it might block plants from sunlight while in another it shelters them from northern winds. Fences, your neighbor's mature Douglas fir trees, a stone wall, or a covered courtyard each can create an area that's slightly cooler or warmer than your "official" garden zone.

The area near a sunny, south-facing wall can be warmer than exposed areas on the other side of your house. Here's where a bright yellow–flowering flannel bush (*Fremontodendron californicum*, Zones 8–10), typically seen thriving in California gardens, might happily grow against a brick house in Portland or Seattle.

If you're in love with marginally hardy plants, try growing them in the warmest microclimate in your garden, such as a sheltered spot with reflective heat. Warmer zones can also exist at the top of a slope, since warm air rises.

Likewise, if you want to make sure plants can endure the most chilly, exposed areas of your landscape, plant durable choices there that can withstand much colder zones. As you observe and identify your garden's microclimates, you'll begin to fine-tune your plant choices. Just be realistic—and don't ask too much of tropical beauties if you really don't have a cozy spot to grow them.

▲ ▼ ▲ ▲ ▼ ▲ ▼ ▼ ▲ ▼ ▲ ▼ ▲ ▼ ▲ ▼

ZONAL DENIAL

Northwest gardeners—and those who have adopted the idea of zonal denial in other temperate regions, such as England—credit Sean Hogan, owner of Portland's Cistus Nursery, for coining the term. Hogan's admiration for and experience in growing plants from South Africa, New Zealand, Australia, and desert regions led him to incorporate many of them into his Northwest garden and nursery displays—with dramatic and exotic results.

To Hogan, the idea of zonal denial has been misinterpreted from his original meaning. "The real concept of zonal denial doesn't really have anything to do at all with growing things that aren't adapted to your climate." He coined the phrase as a garden design concept: "It's basically the idea that you can create whatever atmosphere you want with plants that are well-adapted to the climate you garden in."

But like many popular trends, the notion of zonal denial has been adopted by others and adapted to fit their purposes. A second meaning has emerged for gardeners who've experienced sometimes disappointing and other times exhilarating attempts to seek out and grow plants normally limited to milder winter hardiness zones than those in which they garden.

And while Hogan calls it a misconception, many gardeners now use zonal denial to describe their addiction to enchanting plants not quite hardy enough to grow in their backyard zone. Still, experimentation rewards effort if you capitalize on your garden's microclimates. What else accounts for the increasing presence of Jurassic Park–like tropical, exotic, and semihardy plants showing up in Northwest gardens? "What's the worst that can happen?" zonal denialists ask. The answer is that the plants die, are put on the compost pile, and eventually help feed other plants.

An Internet search yields numerous homegrown references to zonal denial. More than 100 citations pop up, offered by everything from flower show Web sites to horticultural chat rooms. Here is one of my favorite comments on zonal denial, from Thomas Hobbs, the Vancouver, British Columbia–based author of *Shocking Beauty* (Tuttle Publishing, 1999): "Through zonal denial we extend the range of plant selections we can use to achieve dramatic effect . . . this form of escapism goes back to Victorian times at least. I'm an adherent of zonal denial. Although I live in Zone 8, I pretend I'm in Zone 9 or 10. After all, don't many gardeners?"

Try growing a plant labeled outside your hardiness zone and see what happens. Create your own zonal reality by understanding the microclimates in your garden. A sheltered spot protected from the north winds, such as a south- or west-facing concrete wall, can be degrees warmer than exposed windy areas along the north side of your property. Warmer zones can exist at the top of a slope, where air rises. If you live in Zone 7 but are enamored with a plant recommended for Zone 9, go ahead and select a unique microclimate—a sheltered or sunny area—and grow it.

This type of experimentation takes a certain bold, confident attitude. What else accounts for gardeners east of the Cascades keeping their Zone 5 roses alive (with a little help from mulch) in freezing winters? You may fool yourself into believing that your iffy plants will survive a cool, wet winter. You may only enjoy their fleeting presence for two or three milder growing seasons before a brutal winter freeze, but it will be a gratifying experiment nonetheless!

▲ ▼ ▲ ▲ ▼ ▲ ▼ ▲ ▼ ▲ ▼ ▲ ▼ ▲ ▼

ECOSYSTEMS
of the
PACIFIC NORTHWEST
Dual Personalities

Climate, topography, and geology determine our gardening success or failure. Thanks to the north-south "wall" created by the 700-mile-long Cascade Mountain Range (which runs from southern British Columbia to northern California), our region is dramatically divided between the humid, maritime (west) side and the semiarid intermountain (east) side. Precipitation varies from about eight inches per year in the drier central area east of the Cascades to as much as two hundred inches per year in Washington's Olympic rain forests and the upper west slopes of Oregon's coastal range.

For gardeners, this is like living on one side or the other of the former Berlin Wall, because we have a limited common language when it comes to choosing plants. Sandwiched between the Cascades and the Pacific coast, there is a 100- to 150-mile-wide strip that's marked by relatively mild climates where moisture-loving plants are at home and west-facing pockets are like the Mediterranean region. The large area east of the Cascades and west of the Rocky Mountains, known as the inland and intermountain regions of British Columbia, Washington, Oregon, and northern California, offers two seasonal extremes: warmer extended summers and colder drier winters.

Rainfall

Remember the big panic in the 1990s about El Niño and how it was going to change life as we knew it? Everyone was worried that warmer, wetter winters, followed by excessive flooding, would make for impossible conditions for farms and gardens, not to mention put a burden on our region's wastewater infrastructure. While that extreme trend hasn't played out, it does seem that unpredictable Northwest climate patterns have turned us into avid weather-watchers. We record temperature highs and lows, and we faithfully check our rain gauges and note how the sunlight tracks through our garden—all with the hope of better understanding the weather.

Now we welcome rain, especially if it follows an unusually dry summer and fall. We've turned into sky-watchers, thanks to prolonged dry spells, below-normal rainfall, and water conservation concerns. I predict we'll spend the next decade trying to capture as much of our winter rain for use in the summer as we possibly can. I will address some of the best ideas for doing so in the next chapter.

Sunshine or Clouds

Think about your garden's place in the world. Is it in full sun, full shade, part-sun or -shade? What do those sun-exposure requirements really mean on plant tags? When a tag reads "Full Sun," it's referring to six hours or more of sunlight; "Shade" means a plant can grow with fewer than three hours of direct sunlight. In between is "Part Shade," which means a range of four to five hours of sun daily.

Lately, I've noticed that many passionate gardeners take creative license with these guidelines. A speaker at a Northwest Hardy-Plant Study Weekend recently pointed out that the label indicates the light exposure that worked for the original grower or nursery. However, that doesn't mean it's the *only* light exposure that works for a plant!

In the spirit of zonal denial, perhaps we can come up with a new term: light denial. Many shade-loving plants can handle morning sun. Alternately, there are sun-lovers that grow well in the shade, but they may not bloom as prolifically. When it comes to container gardening, I throw out all those sun/shade guidelines and just place my potted plants where I like. If a perennial needs shade, but it's a variegated beauty that I must have for my sunny patio containers, then I try it. Unless you experiment, you're in the dark when it comes to knowing what works and what doesn't. Besides, your plants will let you know what they can handle. After two summers watching the tiny citron leaves of my ghost bramble (*Rubus cockburnianus* 'Aureum') turn crispy brown in a bed that's situated in full sun, the light bulb has finally come on! It's not happy there—and I'm moving this weird, thorny shrub to a border that doesn't get much direct afternoon sunlight.

Temperature Trends

It used to be that I had to replace my New Zealand flax every spring because it seemed too tender for Seattle winters. But for the past five or six years, whether in the ground or in pots, those spiky purple blades have soared through January and February with no problem. This single phenomenon is to me a metaphor for what's going on with weather patterns in our region.

Increasingly balmy winters may signal subtle global warming trends. Take advantage of the rising mercury by experimenting with plants that are one or two zones above your typical range. Just be prepared for Mother Nature to sneak in and surprise you with a chilly winter one of these years.

Natural Topography

Even though I mutter obscenities every time I have to haul buckets of compost up the thirty steps from the curb to my garden, the hilly topography of our region is truly a blessing. Who wants a completely flat garden when the alternative is a sloping area? If you think I'm crazy, consider the benefits of a hillside garden.

Enjoy viewing many plants at once, and play around with varying plant forms and heights. Not all of the taller varieties have to go in the back when you're gardening on a slope. Incorporate fabulous alpine and rock-garden plants into an embankment, selecting the plants that trail, creep, and spread to have their way with the topography. They're happiest here anyway, so encourage their presence in your landscape.

Take advantage of the wonderful drainage offered by a sloped area of the garden too. If you want to grow a finicky plant that requires good drainage, let gravity do the work for you, as everything from irrigation to rainwater will more readily wick away from its roots.

If you aren't blessed with a hillside, create one. Even a small raised rockery offers varied levels. Mimic your favorite part of nature—be it a woodland trail, a beachfront bank, or a mountain meadow—by adding rocks, trees, and shrubs that suggest the Northwest's diverse topography. I'm particularly impressed with gardeners who use berms (mounded areas of soil that elevate eye-catching specimens and break up flat areas—not to mention provide much-desired drainage).

The green Pacific Northwest has conifers, mountain snowpack, and moist air systems to thank for its verdant reputation. Our beloved Douglas firs and western red cedars provide an evergreen backdrop that complements the orna-mental trees, shrubs, perennials, bulbs, and vines you can grow in the garden. I'm a big fan of conifers, choosing them for their brilliant new spring growth, steadfast summer struc-ture, and excellent fall and winter performance. If you're forced to remove a mature evergreen tree from the garden because it's overgrown or diseased, be sure to fill its place with another evergreen, perhaps a new cultivar that offers silvery blue, golden, or chartreuse needles.

Taking Inventory

Get to know and understand your garden's topography. In doing so, you'll make better choices about placement of plants and structures. Be an explorer in your own backyard.

Take note of how the sunlight travels through your landscape. Which areas receive full sun throughout the day, part of the day, or not at all? Are the shady areas completely shaded or do they enjoy filtered or dappled light? What areas receive no sun at all? You might find it helpful to draw a rough map of your yard.

My home faces east and I've learned that the sunlight doesn't even move past the roof of my two-story home, creating shade from the house's shadow, until 2:00 P.M., even during winter. That means I can't put "Shade" plants in the entry garden, since in spring and summer they have as much as eight hours of direct morning and early afternoon sunlight. Thus, no lovely hostas. On the other hand, it is a fabulous location for roses because the earlier light and warmth seems to keep the foliage dry and free from black spot.

Observe changes that are out of your control. These can include a neighbor's trees or construction activity. What once was my successful shade border has been dramatically changed into a row of crispy astilbes and a wrinkled gunnera, thanks to the construction of a new home next door. The project removed several old yew trees, dramatically changing the scene in our garden by letting southwestern sunlight pour on in.

Watch the climate patterns. Observe how wind travels through your landscape. If you're in an exposed area, you'll want to choose durable plants that can handle regular buffeting from strong gusts of wind. Alternately, use the areas where your roof overhangs or the corner between a deck and the house to shelter tender plants from the elements.

Watch how your property drains. Our rain tends to come in prolonged and steady falls, rather than sudden and urgent downpours. This is better for the landscape, helping the soil absorb water at a regular rate. However, during a period of chronic rain, look for the areas of your garden that aren't draining well and devise a solution. We used to call the grassy pathway south of our home "Mud Land." I have vivid memories of my husband's efforts one rainy Thanksgiving Day, digging what he considered to be drainage trenches along the sides of that path. Eventually, we accepted that drainage was horrible on this side of the home, thanks to serious compaction during construction. Out went the sod; in went three inches of crushed gravel. On top of the gravel we've placed an inviting row of two-inch-thick bluestone pavers as a lovely pathway that's not in the least bit soggy. And what fun I had choosing moisture-loving ground covers to thrive alongside the path.

▲ ▼ ▲ ▲ ▼ ▲ ▼ ▲ ▼ ▲ ▼ ▲ ▼ ▲ ▼

PRACTICAL WISDOM FOR NORTHWEST GARDENERS
Mary Robson is a savvy and sensible Northwest gardener who knows how to make the most of limited natural resources. We've enjoyed many years of her advice as the *Seattle Times* "Practical Gardener" columnist. And, as King County's (recently retired) Washington State University Extension agent, Mary has helped thousands of gardeners learn how to cope with our region's challenging soil and tricky rainfall (or lack thereof).

Some of Mary Robson's Observations:
Pay attention to where you garden. Learn about your garden locally, the way you learn about your community. "Hang around and watch it happen," Mary advises.

Observe weather patterns. Northwest gardeners are experiencing myriad changes in temperature and rainfall, much of which is hard to predict. Because increasingly dry weather coincides with our primary growing period (May 1 to October 1), we need to change our attitudes about lush, green lawns. We need to reprioritize our list of favorite plants, choosing those that can adapt to varying conditions throughout the year. Mary posed this question: "When you buy a plant in the spring, start asking yourself how you are going to get the plant to survive the summer?"

Plant for year-round interest. "We have a stronger

desire to enjoy our gardens throughout the year," Mary noted. For some good plant suggestions, see "Ideas for a Drought-Tolerant Perennial Garden" on page 62.

Resist those urges to grow everything. Because we enjoy temperate winters, Mary thinks Northwest gardeners are like passionate cooks. We are inspired by a tasty looking recipe, the ingredients are readily available, and we can whip up a fabulous meal. It's relatively easy to find an array of awesome plants (those great "ingredients") so we don't always stop to consider which ones will succeed in our gardens without demanding excess resources, such as constant summer irrigation. Zonal denial is a fun concept, but, asks Mary, "How well do all these exotic, nonnative plants fit into our landscapes?"

Harvest water. Mary bit the bullet and invested nearly $2,000 in a 1,500-gallon cistern for her retirement home in Port Townsend on Washington's Olympic Peninsula. She plans to "harvest" winter water. "I have done some pretty crazy things to save water," she confides. Made for large western ranches and farms, her new cistern goes a long way beyond the fifty-five-gallon barrel so many of us use to catch free rainfall.

Make smart choices. You don't need to grow picture-perfect tomatoes when the more flavorful ones are oddly shaped. And if you don't love the plant, there's no sense in growing it just because it's drought tolerant.

▲ ▼ ▲ ▲ ▼ ▲ ▼ ▲ ▼ ▲ ▼ ▲ ▼ ▲ ▼

SOIL:
THE CRUEL TRUTH

It was one of those painful heart-to-heart talks. My long-time landscaping buddy, Karen, actually had to take me out to lunch in order to break the news: "Your new property is one tough square of heavy clay soil. You can't have a garden without serious intervention."

My visions of growing a glorious oasis that surrounded our new home were instantly dashed as I realized I couldn't dig hole one without improving that clay soil. I remembered reading about all those old famous English gardeners who put 95 percent of their attention into making good soil ... and 5 percent into the pretty part of gardening.

Soon, with Karen's help, I became an expert on "clay-enhancement," trying an array of products that help turn tough soil into tolerable tilth. I started small. How else can you do it without feeling depressed at the prospect of such backbreaking work? On my first Mother's Day in our new home, my husband, Bruce, gave me the gift of his labor, renting a rototiller to dig up what is now my entry garden filled with David Austin roses, hydrangeas, salvias, and hardy geraniums. Once he broke apart all that tough and compacted clay dirt, I went to work, double-digging and incorporating several bags of that miracle product: ClayBuster. Even if it was worthless, I had to try to improve my soil with something so well branded. Mixed into the wretched native soil, Clay-Buster beefed up the overall texture, allowing for more air pockets to help water drain through it and roots to spread. We planted the first three 'Abraham Darby' roses that May and I was one happy customer when they bloomed a month later. That was in 1998—and I'm still convinced my roses are doing well thanks to that initial dose of ClayBuster. Annual applications of organic mulch are helping the soil's health as well.

Later, when we tackled the backyard, we fed the clay soil with twenty yards of a product called GroCo, rototilling it into the native dirt. A by-product of Metro King County's water treatment plant, GroCo is a compound that's mixed with sawdust, so it's dry and lightweight enough to be blown in. Many large Northwest municipalities offer similar products from their yard-waste programs. Having a topsoil company handle the project was a welcome relief. Importing large volumes of GroCo using huge blowers was much preferred to hauling it in buckets up those thirty steps.

What's Soil Got to Do with It?

Here's the dirt on dirt—soil performs many essential functions important to gardeners. Their purposes include

- **Regulating water** – Soil helps determine where rain, snowmelt, and irrigation water go. Water and anything dissolved in it (fertilizer, toxins, etc.) flow over the land and into or through the soil.
- **Sustaining life** – Animals and plants rely on soil. The diversity and productivity of living things are soil dependent.
- **Filtering potential pollutants** – The minerals and microbes in soil are responsible for filtering, buffering, and detoxifying organic and inorganic materials.
- **Delivering nutrients** – Carbon, nitrogen, phosphorus, and many other nutrients are stored, transformed, and cycled through soil.

Determining Your Soil Health

You don't need to be a soil scientist to understand the nature of the soil in your garden. Get the dirt on your dirt—it will explain how water will move through the landscape, how much water the soil can hold, what kind of environment your plants' roots will have, and what kind of nutrients are present.

Quick Soil Tests

Determine soil type (hand test) – Start by grabbing a handful of soil and squeezing, then open your hand. Does the soil stay balled up as if you had tightened your hand around pie dough and turned it into a lump? If so, you have clay soil. Or, does the soil fall apart and sift through your fingers, falling to the ground? That is sandy soil. The obvious goal is finding soil that's somewhere in-between—once your hand opens, a finely-textured, partially moist pile of dirt smiles back at you and lets you know you've been blessed with wonderful loam.

Evaluate soil moisture (dig-and-fill test) – Dig a hole about six inches deep and six inches wide. Look at and feel the material you remove from the hole to see how moist or dry it is and whether it contains any sand, gravel, clay, or organic matter such as decomposed leaves. Fill the hole with water and observe how quickly the water soaks into the ground. If the soil soaks the water up so fast you can't fill the hole entirely, then you have very well-drained (probably sandy) soil. On the other hand, if that hole is still filled with water after a couple hours, you definitely have poorly drained soil. Try this test in a variety of areas of your property to see if conditions are the same throughout.

Soil Texture

The following definitions of soil texture will help you: most landscapes have a combination of soil types and most gardens require some assistance in order to have productive, healthy soil.

Clay soil – The size of clay particles is the smallest of any component in soil, less than .002 mm. Closely packed, these particles comprise a heavy, sticky, often soggy growing medium. Clay soil absorbs water slowly, causing plant roots to sit in standing water. Because clay soil also drains slowly, it often retains cooler temperatures long into spring.

You can improve clay soil by adding organic matter such as compost, planting mixes, or well-rotted manure. The organic matter enhances the ability for oxygen and water to move freely through the amended clay soil and helps increase the available nutrients in the soil.

Sandy soil – Sandy soil holds few nutrients, in part because sand particles are the largest component in the soil, ranging from .05 to 2 mm, and thus nutrients and water flow right through it. Improve sandy soil by supplementing it with organic material, which provides and stores the nutrients plants need and retains moisture in the root zone. You can improve sandy soil over time by simply topping the soil with organic compost periodically.

Loamy soil – A rare commodity in the Northwest, loamy soil is clearly the best type for gardeners—a combination of sand, silt, clay, and organic matter (decomposed leaves, bark, or manure). Loam not only readily absorbs water, it also retains it. It's that "perfect" soil that we assume is universal until we dig into our own backyard and learn that all soils aren't equal!

Testing and Analysis

Don't let your eyes glaze over when talking about soil pH. It doesn't have to be as complicated as rocket science, and you don't have to spend a fortune to find out what you have. West of the Cascades, most Pacific Northwest soils are slightly acidic. That is why rhododendrons, azaleas, and their relatives are content in many of our gardens. Van Bobbitt, horticulture instructor at South Seattle Community College, wisely advised, '"When in doubt, you can assume that most plants used in Northwest gardens are likely to prefer a slightly acidic soil." In general, soils in wet regions are acidic, while soils in arid regions are alkaline. Gardeners east of the Cascades may notice that their soil is slightly alkaline to neutral.

Soil pH

Where your soil falls on this continuum indicates the acidity or alkalinity of soil, measured on a pH scale of 0 to 14. Starting from 7 as the neutral midpoint and moving toward 0, the soil is increasingly more acidic. Moving from 7 up to 14, the soil is increasingly more alkaline or basic.

Soil pH has a great effect on the solubility of nutrients and minerals. Fourteen of the seventeen essential plant nutrients are obtained from the soil, but before plants can use any nutrient, it must be dissolved in a solution. Most minerals and nutrients are more soluble, thus more available, in acidic soils than in neutral or slightly alkaline soils. Most soil pH levels fall between 4 and 8 and generally, a pH range of approximately 6 to 7 promotes the most readily available plant nutrients. Luckily, there's some wiggle room in these ranges; many plants will grow happily as long as the soil is slightly acidic.

You can always check a general horticultural reference book to determine which plants grow well in higher pH (such as cacti and succulents, which prefer mildly alkaline soils, to about 7.5 pH) or lower pH (such as the aforementioned rhododendrons and azaleas, along with ferns and camellias, which require acidic pHs between 4.5 and 5.5). Or, have fun with your hydrangeas, which tolerate a wide pH range, but change their flower colors depending on the soil (flowers become blue in acidic soil and pink in alkaline).

Old-timers used to taste their soil to determine its pH. Sweet-tasting soil meant it was alkaline; sour-tasting soil was acidic. However, that's not the most scientific method. If you really want to know the pH of your soil, use a home test kit or send a sample to a lab for an in-depth analysis. Some tests include an analysis of soil nutrients and sometimes give suggestions for amendments. To find resources for soil testing, check with your local Cooperative Extension Service. Many local nurseries and garden centers also offer soil-testing services (see "Gardening Resources" for contact information).

Tricking Mother Nature

Once you've determined the general pH of your soil, figure out how to get it close to neutral or slightly acidic. It's an ongoing process, so be flexible with the effort and forgiving with the results. The most useful way to neutralize your soil is to start adding an annual or twice-yearly layer of organic compost to your garden. You can make your own or find a local source that will deliver quality decomposed matter. Remember, if you're spending gobs of money on exciting new plants but you haven't addressed soil health, you're going to be disappointed. One of my trial-and-error gardening friends shared this lament recently: "The mistake I made was jumping right over building a good soil foundation that would support my plants and starting my garden without it." Learn from his true confession and get down and dirty with your soil. Feed the soil and it will feed the plants.

Drainage Dos and Don'ts

You can learn a lot about drainage by just watching your garden during the rainy season or when you water. Once you've done the dig-and-fill test described on page 22, you'll know the spots in your garden that are "drainage-challenged." I lost a beautiful Hinoki cypress because I didn't do that. After the plant turned brown in one year, even though I religiously watered it, I pulled it up out of the hole to discover that the small ball of roots had rotted. Here was a case where no amount of amendment would help improve the drainage—it was a tough, concretelike corner next to a porch. I really wanted a lovely conifer to punctuate that corner, so I found a twenty-four-inch cedar box, stained it to match the porch, and placed it over that spot of clay soil. Today a very happy dwarf conifer grows there, receiving adequate water while growing in soil that drains properly.

Tip

ADD TEXTURE TO SOIL AND IMPROVE DRAINAGE
When you're planting, incorporate one part organic compost with one part native soil (what you just dug out of the hole).

If you can't dig up (or mechanically till) an entire section of clay soil, add two inches of fine mulch or organic compost over the top once or twice a year. In the long term, this is the single best technique for improving the makeup of clay soil.

When you dig a planting hole, make a little mound at the base of the hole. Place the plant's root-ball on the mound, turning the area around it into a "moat." Sprinkle an inch or two of fine crushed rock in the moat before packing soil around the plant. You have accomplished two neat tricks to avoid root rot. First, planting on a mound slightly elevates the root-ball above the clay soil. Second, the crushed rock helps wick water away from the plant's crown, thereby improving drainage.

Design for Drainage

Having interviewed dozens of talented landscapers and garden designers over the years, I've been inspired to try some of their tricks in my own garden, making decisions about my landscape design with an eye toward drainage. Think about these options while you create or renovate areas of the garden.

Raised Beds – There's nothing better for good drainage than layering twelve to eighteen inches of new soil on top of your less-than-perfect existing dirt. You can use all types of materials to create the form for your raised bed, including recycled rocks or boulders, stacked bricks, pressure-treated timbers (avoid this if you plan to grow edibles or line the bed with thick plastic so that any chemicals can't leach into the soil), or two-by-twelve-inch planks or boards made from recycled plastic. Some of these materials last forever; others (such as the planks) may last for ten years before showing signs of degradation. The wood material tends to work best for linear beds—squares and rectangles that suggest production gardens for edibles and cut flowers. Stones and bricks lend themselves to organic shapes that curve through the garden or for creating an island bed in the center of a lawn. What you have to remember is that with watering and disruption, the topsoil will settle over time. This is not a problem because you can top-dress a raised bed with mulch as easily as you do the other beds in your landscape. Be sure to think about access. I have two four-by-eight-foot raised beds along my sunny fence, perfect for my espaliered apple trees, artichokes, and tomatoes. However, since I can't access the beds from both sides, I find that I only use the front half of the bed—the first two feet of planting space that I can reach. Needless to say, I leave my low-maintenance trees and taller dahlias at the back of the beds, since I don't need to reach them as frequently. Typically, three-foot beds are a better option, as are beds that can be accessed from four sides.

French Drains – French drains often emerge as a solution to the problem of moist basements and leaky foundations, but they can also help you address serious drainage problems in the landscape. The technique involves digging an extensive, two-foot-deep trench in the garden, usually following the desired drainage path. Partially fill the trench with gravel (to encourage drainage) and line it with four-inch perforated PVC pipe. The pipe displaces soil and further enhances drainage, and you can wrap the PVC with landscape cloth to keep debris and roots from infiltrating the perforated holes along its sides. Add more gravel and top with soil to bring the trench level with the rest of your garden. It's desirable to connect the drainage pipes to the sewage pipes that capture rainwater from your home's gutters, so that the water seeping into your French drain travels out of your garden rather than down the sidewalk. Some municipal codes restrict the practice of tying your drainage into the storm-water system; check local guidelines before starting the project. Landscape contractors are well equipped to engineer a French drain system, but expect to pay a lot for it.

Berms – To me, a berm is a less-formal raised bed, which allows you to sculpt the earth without using edging material. Some designers use berms in order to relocate soil they've had to excavate from elsewhere in the landscape. I've seen soil piled up over a thick layer of newspaper that's been laid on grass. That's a good solution if you're trying to eradicate large areas of lawn. Berms are also useful for adding a sense of screening or protection, such as along the sidewalk. Visually, the berm can "enclose" your yard. Once you've mounded up a three-foot hill of soil, imagine how tall it will appear once shrubs, ornamental trees, and tall perennials are growing on it. A word about planting. It's the plants—and their roots—that stabilize the berm. Until they are established in this unique, well-drained garden element, keep a close eye out for soil washing off during rain or irrigation. Adding trailing ground cover between the larger plants helps to further stabilize your berm.

Terraces – A terrace allows you to utilize a hilly or steep area. You can turn difficult-to-navigate areas into useful sections that won't give you drainage headaches. If you love the look of a rock garden, select a native stone such as basalt or granite and build your terraces with informal rows. The scale of your home and the plants you want to grow determine the appropriate height of a stone terrace.

Tip **DESIGNING FOR A WELL-DRAINED TERRACE**
To enhance drainage in a terraced garden, first place the rocks or boulders that will create the outside shape of the terrace and then backfill behind the rockery, using smaller crushed rock. Add the planting soil last.

Care and Feeding of Soil

This section could alternatively be called "The Power of Gravity." Everything put into the soil will eventually seep downhill into the watershed. If you value our natural environment—the wonderful lakes, streams, rivers, and bays of the Pacific Northwest—you're probably already sold on organic fertilizers for the garden. Whenever possible, opt for a nonpolluting choice to feed the plants you grow in your soil.

Like favorite remedies for the common cold, opinions about the best soil amendments for Northwest gardens are highly personal. Through trial and error, asking other gardeners for suggestions, and quizzing the experts at your local nursery, you'll find some good options. Here is a short primer on commercial soil amendments. It is helpful when nurseries line up samples of their bagged product choices, open at the top with a hand scoop. That way you can actually feel, smell, and compare the difference between something as enticing as mushroom compost or as smelly as chicken manure. See pages 122–123 in the "Gardening Resources" section for additional information.

Amendments

Compost is the great melting pot of the gardening world, as there are numerous ingredients that can blend together to create an excellent product. Organic material that makes its way into commercial compost includes "clean green" yard waste, sawdust, composted mushrooms, and more. Become a label reader to see what ingredients you're most comfort-able with. The texture of compost is very similar to good, loamy soil. But don't be tricked into thinking it's a replacement for soil. Compost doesn't have the varied minerals to sustain long-term growth of plants.

Manures – Chickens and steer from local farms can do their part to enrich and nourish your garden. You can buy bagged farm manure, order it in bulk from a nearby supplier, or grab a pickup truck and dig your own from a reputable farmer. If you go the latter route, make sure the manure is well rotted before putting it on your beds. There's a visible (and pungent) difference between fresh animal manure and a pile of aged manure. The term *well rotted* generally refers to manure that has aged at least one year.

Planting mixes – You'll be surprised how diversified this range of products has become, offering gardeners plant-specific soil mixes with additives intended for bedding plants (such as annuals), acid-loving woody plants (such as azaleas and rhododendrons), vegetables, bulbs, roses, and more. These soil amendments can be mixed into your native soil or used as mulchlike topdressings.

General-purpose fertilizer – Sometimes it is simplest to opt for the one-size-fits-all transplanting food for uniformity and convenience. When planting a large bed, it's nice to have one bag and one scoop and just dump a cup of something such as Whitney Farms Smart Start into the hole. The only problem is that dogs and other pets love the taste and smell of this stuff. While organic fertilizer isn't harmful to animals, it may be wise to keep your pets indoors for a few days or they may dig into new plantings just to get to the intoxicating treat at the bottom of your planting hole.

Tea, anyone? – If you've visited a specialty nursery, read a popular gardening magazine, or attended one of our region's great garden shows, you've undoubtedly heard about compost tea. Like any hot concept, this one has its roots in a tried-and-true practice. Liquid compost concentrates for plants, lawns, and soil started back in the olden days when farmers steeped manure to pour on their crops. Compost tea has recently been brushed up, polished off, and turned into a consumer product you can buy at local garden centers.

Although I've tried compost tea, I'm not a regular user, mainly because I have a busy family and an inconsistent gardening schedule: those who swear by compost tea seem most successful because they make it themselves and apply it regularly to their garden. Making compost tea requires brewing equipment, but it is worth it to see the fruits of your labor. Many specialty nurseries have brewers on-site and they encourage compost-tea customers to bring their own one-gallon milk jugs for filling at a nominal cost. A designer I know sells her freshly-brewed compost tea at a farmer's market in her community each Saturday. See pages 104–105 for more information on compost tea.

Topsoil – If you're in the market for custom-made topsoil, numerous companies specialize in concocting the right mixture for your particular garden need. For example, a three-way mix includes loam, peat, and compost that are processed through a half-inch screen. In addition, there are also two-way mixes, five-way mixes, a topdressing mixture for lawns, a mixture of half sand and half mulch, and more. A good topsoil provider will help you determine the best mixture for your landscape. When in doubt, I always go for the three-way mix. It's a good option for ornamental gardens and seems to balance out the native soil, whether it's mostly clay or mostly sand.

Mulches

Many people (myself included) are confused as to what mulch is: people use the term in different ways. Organic mulch, which is preferable as it will eventually break down and feed the soil, provides a layer of protection that retains water and suppresses weeds in the landscape. There is such an array of materials that can be used as mulch that you may choose to use one type of mulch in one area of the garden and another in a different space. It's a matter of personal choice.

Some people like to adorn their soil with huge chunks of bark or wood chips. I prefer a low-key layer of finely shredded bark that almost looks like soil itself. We should appreciate how lucky we are that there is an abundant supply of fir and hemlock for this purpose right here in the Pacific Northwest.

This is not so in most other regions of the country. You can order fine, medium, or coarse mulch mixes from most providers. There are also specialty mulches available. One I've begun using, called "screened comp-mulch," is a mixture of composted sawdust and cow/steer manure processed through a half-inch screen. Not only does it have a nice brownish-red color, it contains a good supply of nutrients and aids in water retention.

Exotica – To seasoned gardeners, these suggestions won't come as a surprise, but as to a beginning gardener, these soil amendments may seem unusual. First of all, check out your local zoo or animal farm to inquire about buying animal manure. In Seattle, there's now a lottery system for Woodland Park Zoo's famed "Zoo Doo." Doesn't your garden deserve the by-product of giraffes, elephants, and the like? Another exotic mulch is coffee grounds. Coffee devotees need go no farther than their nearby café to get this remnant of the caffeine addicted. Usually free for the taking, coffee grounds are excellent nitrogen-rich amendments for your home compost pile and can be used as a mulch. Spreading coffee grounds directly on the soil is not advised if you have pets around.

You may want to incorporate the grounds into your soil as a nutrient rather than using the material as a mulch. This discourages curious pets from getting a potentially toxic jolt of caffeine.

The Bottom Line

If you're into instant gratification, remember this wonderful saying from Gandhi: "There is more to life than increasing its speed."

Nothing could be truer in a garden. Slow down and acquaint yourself with the patch of earth you call home. Get on your knees and look closely at the soil. Run your fingers through it. Watch how plants grow—both the successes and the failures. Observe what happens in every season. Benefit from time spent in the garden. I'm an advocate of squeezing in gardening for any length of time. If I have ten minutes to wait for the pasta to cook, I'm sneaking out the back door to pull a few weeds, deadhead a few spent blooms, or water my containers.

If you're well into making a garden and you think that perhaps the condition of your soil is holding you back, don't be discouraged. It's never too late to start nourishing your soil. You don't have to dig everything up and start over. Simply begin adding healthy mulches and fertilizers on a seasonal basis. There's more to a beautiful garden than meets the eye—and a lot of it is underground.

▲ ▽ ▲ ▲ ▽ ▲ ▽ ▲ ▽ ▲ ▽ ▲ ▽ ▲ ▽

THE SOIL DOCTOR

Howard Stenn has incorporated the word "bed digger" into his e-mail address. For someone who splits his professional life between designing drought-tolerant gardens and advising Northwest municipalities on water conservation and soil quality, it's a fitting nickname.

Stenn has combined the two specialties as author of a valuable series of guides, The Natural Lawn and Garden—Healthy Landscapes for a Healthy Environment. Sponsored by the Saving Water Partnership, the series is comprised of five booklets, including *Growing Healthy Soil*, which you can download free from the Web site (www.savingwater.org).

Stenn has a pragmatist's way of balancing forces that seem at odds with one another. Although we have limited natural resources with which to garden, water is one of the most precious. Yet, we want to be surrounded by abundant, beautiful, lush gardens. Can we possibly save water and still have a verdant garden?

Stenn urges people to start from the ground up. Soil isn't sexy, but it is essential to your success as a gardener. So many gardeners begin planting in soil that's been disturbed by time, construction, or renovation. He maintains that if you invest in improving that bad soil before ever buying a pretty plant, you can eventually nourish a beautiful—and healthy—garden.

He debunks the myth that all Northwest soil is clayey. "People often mischaracterize their soils," Stenn states. "People tell me they have horrible clay soil, but I see sandy soils as much as I see clay soils. Often what people think is clay is just dry or compacted fine-sandy loam, which is hard to dig."

According to Stenn, there seem to be equal quantities of poor clay soil in the lower shoreline areas and on slopes, and poor sandy soil on ridges and many islands in Puget Sound.

Compost is an excellent amendment for both extremes. He recommends mixing several inches of compost into sandy soil when starting a new garden, adding another inch or two annually. If you have clay soil, choose compost that contains more woody material, such as a mixture of manure composted with sawdust or bark.

When it comes to choosing mulch, Stenn is opinionated, warning that repeated layers of ornamental ground bark can be damaging to gardens: "It actually sheds water and inhibits a lot of plant growth," he cautions. "Using arborist chips [finely-shredded wood chips often available free from arborists] is a smarter choice. They look more natural, support more soil life, and let water through." If you can't find arborist chips, ask your local supplier for bark that's been composted with sawdust.

Healthy soil is an investment in your garden, one that will help cut your water bills, improve the overall water quality of a region, and even reduce backbreaking work such as weeding and digging. Stenn shares three tips for successfully growing healthy soil:

- Before planting, amend the soil throughout the entire planting area with compost.
- Mulch existing plantings with compost, leaves, grass clippings, or woody mulches.
- When you need to feed plants, use natural organic and slow-release fertilizers.

▲ ▼ ▲ ▲ ▼ ▲ ▼ ▲ ▼ ▲ ▼ ▲ ▼ ▲ ▼

▲ ▼ ▲ ▲ ▼ ▲ ▼ ▲ ▼ ▲ ▼ ▲ ▼ ▲ ▼

TRUE GRIT: GRAVEL GARDENING

Never before have I felt such an urgency to buy crushed stone in large quantities then when I heard Portland grower Maurice Horn give his "True Grit" lecture at the annual Northwest Hardy-Plant Study Weekend.

Horn, an experienced gardener, plantsman, and co-owner of Joy Creek Nursery in Scappoose, Oregon, has developed a singular method of coping with the concretelike clay soil conditions so many of us Northwest gardeners face. The answer is in 1/4–10 gravel. This number refers to the size of the stones: 1/4–10 mix means the crushed basalt rock is reduced to pieces that are one-fourth inch to one-tenth inch in size. No fine dust particles are left in the mixture.

"Gravel has become my mantra," Horn proclaimed to an audience of nearly 500. Many Northwest gardeners are hindered by the universal challenge of poorly drained soil. According to Horn, clay is the culprit. Clay can be blamed for everything from anaerobic conditions, in which there is no oxygen exchange at the root level, to perpetual winter wetness, which threatens to cause root rot for the toughest of plants.

Horn likes to garden with a "true grit" approach. In some areas of the famous display gardens at Joy Creek Nursery, a mixture of 1/4–10 crushed gravel mixed into the native soil helps wick rainfall away from the plants' crowns to protect from rotting. He advises that spreading a ring of gravel around the base of a plant will accomplish the same result. In other areas, such as a lavender path planted with seventy-eight forms of lavender, Horn prefers a two-inch mulch of crushed rock. "Gravel is so inorganic that there is no danger to it rotting woody stems," he advises. "It serves as a great mulch."

Horn counts on his true grit method for tackling what he calls "hell strips," the typically compacted strip of grass between the street and sidewalks in front of urban and suburban homes. "They're dry, hard to water, and usually in full sun," he explains. True grit methods are easy to emulate. They encourage you to try growing an attractive garden in a place where expectations are at their lowest. Horn advises gardeners to forget about tidy beds of woolly thyme and oregano. Try dynamic plantings of trees and shrubs as they can thrive in a hell strip.

Below are Horn's methods for dealing with a hell strip.

1. Lift off the turf.
2. Work in an organic compost that contains plenty of leaf mold into the soil.
3. Double-dig crushed gravel into the new planting medium by systematically digging and turning over rows the width and depth of your spade. The quantity of gravel you use can vary, depending upon the quality of the native soil (some people also incorporate organic compost or topsoil during this step, refilling the rows with a mixture of native soil, compost, and gravel). Horn prefers topdressing the entire area with two inches of gravel and working that into the soil.
4. Once you've added plants to the strip, mulch the entire bed with more gravel.

This may sound like a lot of work, but tackle it the way Horn and his Portland neighbors did. They worked together—like an old-fashioned block party—helping renovate and beautify the strips in front of each other's homes.

▲ ▼ ▲ ▲ ▼ ▲ ▼ ▲ ▼ ▲ ▼ ▲ ▼ ▲ ▼

Hardworking Plants for Pacific Northwest Gardens

Trees

Acer circinatum (vine maple) – Multistemmed small tree that's native to moist soils of the maritime Pacific Northwest. Looks great in natural and woodland settings. Lovely fall color. Zones 6–9.

Acer palmatum (Japanese maple) – A versatile tree with countless cultivars. Plant in a small grove or as a specimen. Great for containers. Zones 6–8.

Cercis canadensis (eastern redbud) – Stunning small tree with heart-shaped foliage. Plant where the sunset provides a glowing backlight. 'Forest Pansy' with reddish leaves is a popular cultivar for smaller gardens. *Cercis occidentalis,* the western redbud, is a drought-tolerant choice. Zones 5–9.

Chamaecyparis obtusa (Hinoki cypress) – Elegant evergreen that requires drainage but can take tough soils. Grows in full sun or part shade. 'Gracilis' is a slender, upright choice for smaller gardens; 'Gracilis Aurea' has golden yellow foliage. Zones 4–8.

Rhus typhina (staghorn sumac) – Performs well in a wide range of climates and soils. Has showy fernlike foliage that turns brilliant orange-red in fall. A good choice for large containers because it tends to spread by suckers. The suckering can be advantageous when planted on a hillside, as the trees help prevent erosion. Zones 3–8.

Shrubs/Vines

Akebia quinata (five-leaf akebia) – Indestructible deciduous vine that can take sun or shade. Interesting leaflets and chocolate-purple spring flowers (which may be why this is also called chocolate vine) with vanillalike fragrance. Zones 5–9.

Nandina domestica (heavenly bamboo) – Bamboolike foliage, with bright red berries in late summer, this durable plant adds texture and interesting form to the garden, not to mention lovely fall color. Nice container choice. Zones 6–9.

Pieris japonica cvs. (Japanese pieris) – Also known as lily-of-the-valley bush or andromeda. Choose from several cultivars with winter-blooming pink, cream, or maroon tassel-like blooms. Elegant foliage; prefers part shade. Zones 6–8.

Roses

SPECIES ROSE

Rosa nutkana (Nootka rose) – Deciduous shrub with single deep-pink flowers in summer and showy red-purple hips during winter. This rose thrives in extremes from Alaska to Northern California. Zones 3–9.

SHRUB ROSES

Two repeat-bloomers that are easy to grow in Northwest gardens. Make an impact with mass plantings.

Rosa 'Bonica' (Bonica rose) – Produces large sprays of rose-pink blooms from spring to autumn. Low, spreading habit. Zones 4–9.

Rosa 'Sally Holmes' (Sally Holmes rose) – Upright shrub with glossy, dark green leaves and many blush-white flowers that bloom from spring to autumn. Zones 5–9.

HEDGE ROSES

Durable roses for foundation, hedge, or border plantings

Rosa 'Iceberg' (Iceberg rose) – Takes poor soil and produces pure white blooms from spring to autumn. Can also be trained as a climber. Zones 5–9.

Rosa rugosa (Rugosa rose) – Tough and hardy species rose with many hybrids. This thorny shrub is often used in exposed sites or as a hedge, with blooms spring to autumn, followed by tomato-red hips. Zones 2–9.

Ornamental Grasses

Calamagrostis x *acutiflora* 'Karl Foerster' (feather reed grass) –
While this upright semi-evergreen grass needs some
irrigation, it performs well in most garden conditions. In
mid- to late summer, this tall grass produces pink-bronze
inflorescences (tassels). Zones 5–9.

Carex spp. (sedges) – Versatile clumping grasslike plant with
many interesting cultivars, mostly evergreen. Prefers moist
soil, but will also tolerate drought conditions. Many carex
bear flower spikes in late spring or summer. Zones 5–9.

Luzula nivea (snowy woodrush) – Evergreen with handsome
wide blades; produces open panicles from mid-spring to
summer. Can take poor soil; prefers full sun. Look for
cultivars with white margins for added interest. Zones 4–9.

Miscanthus sinensis (silver grass) – Clump-forming grasses
that need little care. There are many elegant cultivars with
graceful stems and showy autumn seed heads, such as
'Gracillimus,' 'Morning Light,' and 'Variegatus.' Zones 4–9.

Panicum virgatum (switch grass) – Takes full sun or light shade,
any amount of water, and produces airy blooms that persist
through winter. Zones 5–9.

Perennials

Achillea millefolium (common yarrow) – A favorite of butterflies
and other pollinators, this old-fashioned perennial has
flat-headed flower clusters in shades of yellow, pink,
cream, or red from early to late summer. Takes full sun
and little to moderate water. Zones 3–9.

Sedum spp. (sedum) – An excellent choice for low-maintenance
gardens. Sedums vary from large and stunning ('Autumn
Joy,' a late summer to autumn bloomer) to trailing varieties
that look nice in rockeries or containers throughout
summer and into early autumn. Zones 3–10.

WILD WEATHER and CHANGING CLIMATES

WEATHER WISDOM: SOGGY VERSUS SCORCHED

What's up with the weather anyway? While our relatives and friends from elsewhere in the country tease us about the Northwest's perpetual showers, we gardeners are desperately trying to ration water sources to keep our thirsty plants alive. Then, when it does rain, we worry that the moisture will rot finicky plants' root systems. Does anyone see the irony in this picture?

Local newspapers proclaimed the summer of 2002 "one of the warmest, driest seasons on record." The Seattle area had two straight months of 70° F-plus days, and precipitation between June and August was the lowest since recordkeeping began in 1895. In recent summers, Oregon has experienced much of the same strange weather, with the 2000–01 "water year" (October 1, 2000 to September 31, 2001) among the driest in history.

Conditions from the past few summers have put others and me on guard, changing my attitude about how I use water in the garden and which plants I select. As "water-wise" as we all hope to be in our selection of plants and irrigation practices, there's something horrifying about walking into the backyard in July and realizing that all of the foliage on my established witch hazel shrub has turned brown. It's *possible* that several deep waterings of my mixed-shrub border will still save that glorious 'Jelena' witch hazel. At the very least, I'm cheered by the fact that all the other woody plants in this border are still thriving.

I've gardened in my current Seattle backyard for six years, during which time I've adopted a "survival of the fittest" attitude. This means ripping up all the soaker hoses once plants become established in a particular area of my garden. It's not a bad exercise, because doing so has quickly revealed which plants can handle extended periods of no rain—and which can't survive without weekly douses of water.

However, recent Seattle summers have demanded that we keep closer watch on our thirsty plants and our water usage. I had several one-year-old plantings that really needed supplemental watering. I watched my bimonthly water bills climb to $250 in June/July and August/September. Since I don't have a cistern or rain barrel to fill with large quantities of excess water, I've already begun filling recycled one-gallon milk jugs with water from the basin of our basement dehumidifier. At the very least, this water stockpile will keep my many outdoor containers refreshed next summer.

Nevertheless, the bottom line is that almost all landscapes in the eastern and central areas of Oregon and Washington require summer irrigation every year. West of the Cascades, we can still tinker with our water use, but only because we have sustained rainfall to saturate the soil during the winter months.

Gardening Is an Extreme Sport

No matter where you turn in the Northwest, there are extreme conditions to face. While the Italian-inspired garden of my Yakima friend, Nancy Ellison, is enough to make me forget travel plans to Florence, she reminds me that Yakima experiences about seven inches of precipitation a year—mostly from snowfall. On the west side of the Cascades, we have our own version of "extreme" gardening, with a moderate Mediterranean-like climate that gives us generous winter rains and close to zero precipitation in the summer. The opposite, of course, would be a monsoon climate, with winter drought and summer rain, but who wants that?

How do we help tender plants survive cold and damp winters? How can thirsty plants make it through droughtlike summers? Once you learn the secret recipes for garden survival, you'll enjoy choosing awesome plants and designing successful beds and borders. More important, you'll learn to appreciate the landscape and its beauty without stressing out about your water bill.

Helping Tender Plants Survive Winter

Winter Layering

In fashion, the "layering" concept resonates with those of us who remember 1980s fashion styles. Likewise, hiking enthusiasts dress in layers, which help insulate them when it's cold or wet and help cool them if temperatures rise. Try the same idea with your garden, adding protective layers over tender plants and helping them survive wet and chilly winters.

Organic layering is the smart approach—and you can increase or decrease stratums of mulch, leaves, or branches according to your garden environment. Think of the well-used phrase "putting your garden to bed for the winter." That analogy makes sense—covering root systems, swaddling vulnerable stems and susceptible branches, and making sure everything is braced for whatever winter brings. Humans like to "cocoon" in the cooler season, coming indoors for mugs of hot tea by the fire. Plants need protection and warmth, too.

It's usually not simply cold temperatures that kill plants; it's the combination of persistent *wet* weather with sudden drops below freezing. Here are some great seasonal ideas for staying one step (or layer) ahead of those surprises.

Weeding and cleanup – Once perennials have died back, usually after November 1, cut back spent blooms and all the raggedy foliage. You don't need to do a radical pruning job;

that's better done in early spring. Just tidy up. Prune dead or diseased branches around the base of woody shrubs to allow space for better air circulation. Give your beds, borders, and planting areas a final weeding. Use a cultivator to break up and remove tougher roots. This is very important, especially as an unseasonably warm autumn is likely to jump-start the germination of another round of unwanted weeds. There is no point in mulching if you haven't bothered to remove the weeds the mulch is supposed prevent. If you do thoroughly weed then apply mulch, the "blanket" of mulch will help suppress new weed seeds from taking root in the soil.

Mulching – Not only does mulch give your garden a finished appearance, it also protects plant roots from weather extremes. Consider mulch your garden's security blanket. Some mulches are selected for their ornamental value, such as traditional landscaping bark. Other mulches come straight out of the garden; shredded leaves or evergreen boughs, for example, add a practical and protective cover around the exposed base of trees and shrubs.

Feeding mulches, such as those that contain additional organic matter, will break down during the winter months and deliver microorganisms to the soil while also acting as a weed suppressant. By the time spring arrives, the mulch will have decomposed and enriched the soil beneath. Add mulch around established plantings, approximately one- to three-inches deep, depending on the size of your trees, flowers, or trees. To prevent root or crown rot, leave a one- to six-inch area around the plant's stem free of mulch (the bigger the plant, the wider the mulch-free area). Don't overmulch, as this could suffocate your plants.

Emergency measures – Even with a cleaned-up and layered garden that's ready to face winter, you'll need to stay alert to seasonal surprises. Containers holding tender plants (such as a Zone 8 restio or abutilon) need protection. Dig holes (perhaps in a hidden area of the garden) and sink the pots into the ground. Add additional layers of protection if necessary. Relocate some containers next to the foundation of the house or inside the garage. (Don't forget to water them periodically until temperatures climb.) Wrap trunks of marginal plants with insulating sheets of burlap or landscaping cloth. Two Seattle Tropicalismo gardeners say they protect the trunks of hardy banana trees with bubble wrap, first winding twinkling holiday lights around the trunks for a bit of whimsy.

Take note – Many exotic plants can handle a single night's surprise freeze, so don't panic if the mercury drops into the 20s come January or February. Be sure you quickly respond to nature's whims: add on an extra layer of evergreen boughs to your perennial beds, wrap a blanket of burlap or landscape cloth around a trunk, or haul the containers indoors—as soon as possible.

Helping Thirsty Plants Endure Summer

Saving Water

You don't have to sacrifice your dreams of tending to a beautiful, lush garden just because you fear it will guzzle excessive amounts of water. Instead, try these techniques for quenching your garden's summer thirst.

Sunrise, sunset – Water your plants early in the morning, when it's cool: water won't evaporate as readily as it does in the heat of the afternoon. If the only time you can water is on an evening schedule, keep water off foliage and direct it to the root systems, as water sitting on leaves overnight encourages fungal diseases.

Rainfall watering – Another proven method of water delivery is to irrigate during a light rainfall. As crazy as it sounds, you can maximize the effect of both the rain and the irrigation if you soak beds and borders when the air is already damp.

Deep waters – If you water less frequently, make sure the water sinks deeper into the soil to encourage roots to grow deep, where the soil remains moist longer. Frequent, shallow waterings lead to weaker root systems closer to the surface of the soil. If water pools or puddles, turn your system off until the water soaks into the soil. After that, you can resume watering, if necessary.

Target the soil – Overhead sprinkling is the least efficient way to water the garden. You lose a substantial percentage of the water to evaporation, especially when temperatures climb, and the risk of fungal disease increases if the foliage stays wet too long. Using watering methods that target the root systems—where plants take in moisture—gives the best results. Consider a watering can, soaker hoses, or drip irrigation, all of which can saturate the soil while leaving the foliage dry. Here is a quick primer on types of soil-specific irrigation.

- SOAKER HOSE This product "sweats" water along its entire length. It is best used when covered with two inches of soil or mulch to prevent water from evaporating. Use soaker hoses to thoroughly water dense plantings or rows of plants in the vegetable garden. As a rule, run most soaker hoses for thirty to forty minutes per week. Dig into your soil an hour after watering to check soil moisture depth. If the soil in your plants' root zone is moist throughout, you've watered long enough. Target your irrigation by attaching soaker hoses to solid hoses. This eliminates wasting water in areas that don't need it. I like to use soaker hoses when establishing new plants. Two or three years after planting, I can pull up the soaker hoses and shift to occasional, deep watering.

- DRIP IRRIGATION Drip systems apply water directly to the soil through tiny outlets called emitters or through microsprays plugged into flexible tubing laid on the ground surface and covered with mulch. Drip systems are an efficient way to irrigate your garden, especially if you have irregularly spaced plants or plants that prefer moist foliage. With a little preplanning, it's possible to install such a system, along with a useful timer, over one weekend.

Mulch Holds Moisture

A two- to three-inch layer of organic mulch, such as shredded leaves, finely shredded bark, or organic compost, slows evaporation of moisture in the plant's root area. Mulch shades and cools the soil, in addition to slowing down water runoff. Mulch also enriches plants, building healthy soil as it slowly decomposes.

Choose drought-tolerant plants. Be horticulturally water-smart; resort to "tough love" in the garden. Once a plant is established in the landscape (usually by its third growing season), experiment to see how well it endures the summer without a lot of water. This is difficult. However, when you choose plants known for their drought-tolerant tendencies and maintain a less-frequent watering schedule, you go a long way toward cutting back on excessive water use. Schedule deep irrigation once every two weeks. Low-water-use plants include herbs and varieties from the Mediterranean region. Plants with silvery, hairy, or fuzzy leaves, succulent leaves, leaves with a waxy coating, and plants with long taproots are also generally drought-tolerant. For suggestions, see "Designing a Drought-Tolerant Garden," on pages 60–61 and "Ideas for a Drought-Tolerant Perennial Garden," pages 62–63.

Plant smart. Unless you're willing to spend more on your water bill, don't start your garden at the height of a dry season. New plants require a steady diet of water. Put off major planting projects until fall; this is the Northwest Gardener's best time for planting.

Cut less. If you have a lawn, mow during the coolest part of the day. Leave the clippings on the grass to replenish the soil. In general, mowing causes water loss to your lawn. Raise the height of your mower to two and one-half to three inches. The longer blades of grass will further shade your soil, conserving water and preventing weed germination.

The anti-lawn – Here's a radical idea: remove your grass altogether and replace it with beds of drought-tolerant plants, sturdy ground covers, and inviting paths. Two years ago, a designer friend created a thyme lawn for a client's front garden. This provided areas of soft, textured green growth that are drought tolerant. Like a lawn, the thyme also solves a typical design challenge: providing a verdant, solid plane that complements more complex plantings of trees and shrubs. Additionally thyme is a fragrant, edible, and low-maintenance choice.

Coping with turf – If you must have grass, allow the lawn to go dormant during the dry season. The minute fall's cooler weather and autumn showers arrive, the green lawn will return. You may also consider planting an eco-lawn, available as a regionally appropriate seed mix that produces a lawn needing less water and lower maintenance. Eco-lawn or eco-turf mixtures contain perennial rye grasses blended with a lovely palette of other plants (English daisy, alyssum, and white clover, among other choices). (See page 124 in "Gardening Resources" section for contact information for eco-lawn seed mixes.)

▲ ▼ ▲ ▲ ▼ ▲ ▲ ▼ ▲ ▼ ▲ ▲ ▼ ▲ ▼ ▲ ▼

WHEN TO WATER AND HOW MUCH?

	ANNUALS	TREES, SHRUBS, PERENNIALS	LAWNS
Water WHERE the roots are*	• Most roots are in the top 12 inches of soil, spreading just a short distance from the plant. (Recent transplants and seedlings have shallower roots.)	• Root systems can go down a couple of feet, and may extend two to five times the branch spread.	• Typically 4 to 6 inches deep, and only under areas covered by grass.
SIGNS it is TIME to water	• Soil is dry below the surface. • Evergreen leaves are dull or bronze. (Try not to let plants wilt. Most will be stunted or die if allowed to dry out.)	• Wilted leaves that do not perk up in the evening. • Yellowing deciduous leaves before autumn.	• Dull green color. • Footprints show long after you walk across the lawn. • Difficult to push a screwdriver or trowel into the soil.
WHEN to water and HOW MUCH	• Check soil often to make sure it stays moist 1 to 2 inches below the surface.	• Water needs vary widely by plant and situation; many may not need irrigation a few years after planting in proper conditions. • Refer to gardening books or ask nursery experts about water needs of plants.	• Apply no more than 1 inch of water each week during summer, including rain. • Lawns allowed to turn brown recover better if they get a thorough soaking every month in summer.

* Roots may be shallower or less widespread if soil is compacted or disturbed.
Courtesy Seattle Public Utilities/Saving Water Partnership

▲ ▼ ▲ ▲ ▼ ▲ ▲ ▼ ▲ ▼ ▲ ▲ ▼ ▲ ▼ ▲ ▼

▲ ▼ ▲ ▲ ▼ ▲ ▼ ▲ ▼ ▲ ▼ ▲ ▼ ▲ ▼

HOW LONG SHOULD I WATER?

How LONG to water if I have:	Average depth in your cans after 15 minutes **				
	1/8"	1/4"	1/2"	3/4"	1"
CLAY soil (1X per week*)	2 hrs.	1 hr.	30 min.	23 min.	15 min.
LOAMY soil (2X per week)	1 hr.	30 min.	15 min.	11min.	8 min.
SANDY soil (3X per week)	40 min.	20 min.	10 min.	8 min.	5 min.

* May be split into two or more applications a few hours apart to prevent runoff.

** See "Avoid overwatering" on page 109 for instructions.

Courtesy Seattle Public Utilities/Saving Water Partnership

▲ ▼ ▲ ▲ ▼ ▲ ▼ ▲ ▼ ▲ ▼ ▲ ▼ ▲ ▼

Human Influences

Gardens are altered spaces. When we cultivate the earth, add ornamental and nonnative plants to the landscape, and impose our own idea of beauty to a backyard lot, we are changing the natural environment.

As much as we may want to emulate the natural splendor we see on a hike in the woods or a visit to the ocean or country-side, we can't help but leave our human-imposed choices around the residential garden. There's a price to pay for all these changes—major or subtle. Ripping out trees to improve one's view, shifting earth to create a level lawn, or planting aggressive vines such as English ivy can yield results that are difficult to reverse. If you recognize the potential down-side of your landscaping choices, you can try to meet Mother Nature halfway. Perhaps you can learn how to mimic nature, for example leaving portions of the garden untouched as wildlife habitat or planting like-minded trees, shrubs, and perennials together for optimal use of resources.

The manner in which water responds (trickles, flows, pools, and drains) is one of the first clues that a gardener has altered the topography of a place. I've had to learn this lesson twice in the past six years, as my construction projects and those of my neighbors have disrupted the character of the clay soil that surrounds our foundations—soil that had existed undisturbed for forty years or more. Removing trees, grinding stumps, and regrading areas of the yard have changed the course that rain and irrigation water take.

Ironically, as careful as we have been to layer crushed rock around the foundation and otherwise improve drainage around the house, we still witnessed two inches of water seeping into the basement one summer. At first, I blamed the minor flooding on my twice weekly watering of a new hydrangea collection. However, by the time a record-breaking rainstorm arrived, dropping five inches of water in one day, portions of the basement filled again. Why had this happened when the area had remained dry during five previous winters?

"Water finds its own course," pontificated my wise neighbor Shawn, a contractor who's seen it all. "Water will go where it wants to." After I meditated on his Zen-like pronouncements, I thought about the magic of gravity and the light bulb in my head went on. Water flows downhill toward rivers, lakes, streams, and oceans. If you can harness those courses and redirect the water to where you need it, that's good. If not, instead of fighting it, consider creating a bog garden. In my case, I realized that the recent construction activity adjacent to our home had removed several established trees, leaving underground gaps in the previously impenetrable clay soil. Instead of slowly seeping through the dense earth, rainfall now had a chance to rush straight toward our foundation. We addressed the problem in the form of an expensive new basement drainage system, plus a moisture-sensitive pump that extracts any further water seepage.

Construction and Development

Save yourself a few headaches by staying one step ahead of a construction or maintenance project. Your garden will thank you. Anticipate and expect that whatever can go wrong, will. That rule extends to what you can control (major pruning projects, window washing, minor repairs, and house painting), and what you can't control (the neighbor's new home addition).

In the past four years, every home on my city block has been remodeled, torn down, or rebuilt. There's no denying that each of these projects has improved the aesthetics of the neighborhood, boosting property values. However, these endeavors have also changed microclimates in the gardens surrounding them. Plants that used to be shaded are now exposed to more sun than ever. Plants that once grew in dry areas are now standing in extra water.

One of the best things you can do to reverse the impact of construction is to replace plants that have been removed. Bare soil is susceptible to erosion, which leads to a loss of soil in garden runoff that drains into nearby lakes, rivers, and streams.

By getting roots of new trees and shrubs quickly established, you stabilize the soil and help slow down flooding or water runoff. Additionally, gravel, stones, and boulders integrated into the landscape provide pockets for establishing new plants, especially natives ones. Organic mulches knit everything together to further reduce runoff.

Treemendous Trees

Planting trees is our investment in the future of our gardens. It's a singular gesture that helps fill the inevitable "holes" in the tree canopy. Whether in tiny urban yards, in suburban developments, or in rural areas, the planting of trees suitable for the landscape is one great investment you can make for your garden. Think of the addition of a tree as a four-season bonus. The leafy canopy cools us in the summer, the textured bark and branch forms share beauty and structure in the winter months, and the berries and seeds provide wildlife habitat in autumn and spring.

Water Wasters

Consider getting rid of your continually thirsty plants and opt instead for those that can tolerate low levels of water during a dry summer. When a plant tells you it can't last without constant water, it's time to do what a friend calls "shovel pruning." Toss that water waster into the compost heap.

Are We Experiencing El Niño?

The weather terms El Niño and La Niña have been bandied about frequently. Several research scientists at the University of Washington's Climate Impacts Group put these terms into perspective for the gardening world. Remember that these terms refer to an "increased probability" of warmer or cooler weather, respectively. There's considerable uncertainty when it comes to knowing what type of weather Mother Nature will send our way each year.

El Niño is defined as an ocean weather phenomenon that occurs for a two- to seven-year period, which tends to give us *overall warmer* weather conditions. La Niña is defined as a similar period during which weather is *cooler than normal*. Then there are "neutral" years when we experience a slightly drier-than-normal winter combined with lower snowpack levels in the mountains.

"For gardeners looking at El Niño and La Niña and using them as a factor for planting decisions, you have to remember that they are not permanent states—they shift," advises Dr. Cliff Mass, a University of Washington climatologist frequently heard on KUOW-FM in Seattle. "You wouldn't want to assume you could plant certain tender perennials on reliance of an El Niño forecast alone."

▲ ▽ ▲ ▲ ▽ ▲ ▽ ▲ ▽ ▲ ▽ ▲ ▽ ▲ ▽

TWO EXTREMES: PRECIPITATION AND DROUGHT

A conversation with Dr. Philip Mote, research scientist with the University of Washington's Climate Impacts Group and state climatologist, reveals both the big picture and the finer intricacies of weather influences on gardeners—and our weather-wise coping habits.

Savvy gardeners are in tune with changing seasonal conditions. Once we get a handle on the extremes of rainfall in winter and the dearth of precipitation in summer, we respond accordingly. The moment the weather forecast promises a change in cooler or warmer temperatures, we shift gears. But how can we anticipate overall temperature trends and predict future weather patterns? What's just a weather anomaly and what's really an indicator of wet or dry, cool or warm years to come?

While global climate changes are influenced by many factors, such as greenhouse gases, the swirling flow of the atmosphere can make one region warm and another region cool without changing that average, according to Dr. Mote. "The overall warming of North America is very likely caused by greenhouse gases," he observes. "But the atmosphere has been tremendously capable of redistributing heat." The summer of 2002, for example, was brutally hot in Europe, while in the Pacific Northwest thermometers climbed just "above average." At the same time, the eastern United States was cooler and wetter than average.

Dr. Mote points out that two important variations in the Pacific Ocean influence the year-to-year climate variations in the Pacific Northwest: the tropical El Niño/La Niña phenomenon and the more northerly Pacific Decadal Oscillation (PDO). Depending on their phases, El Niño/La Niña and the PDO nudge the Northwest's winter climate in one of two directions: either toward slightly warmer, drier conditions (1997–98, 2002–03) or slightly cooler, wetter conditions (1998–99).

Since the mid-1990s, the Pacific Northwest has witnessed the PDO's cooler phase. Of course, there have been exceptions—the winter of 2000–01 was drier and warmer than average. Yet, explains Dr. Mote, "The decadal story [decade-by-decade comparison] of the twentieth century was trending toward warmer temperatures in most seasons, and trending toward wetter winters overall."

The region's climate picture indicates a slight shift upward in both winter and summer temperatures. He says, "Everywhere it's warmer." We're talking subtle changes, such as an average increase during the summer months of 1.5° F, and an average increase during winter months of 3° F—over fifty years! "We're more likely to get milder winters and less likely to get colder winters," Mote predicts.

When it comes to water resources—a topic of high concern for everyone in the Northwest, including gardeners—Dr. Mote says he's cautiously optimistic, thanks to the impressive shift toward better stewardship of water resources since the early 1990s. "Even with our population growth in Seattle and the suburbs over the last ten years, the water demand is still lower than the pre-1992 levels," he notes. However, the picture is less rosy in over-allocated basins such as the Klamath region and the Columbia River basin.

As we begin to learn to live with less water and carefully use the water resources we have, we must make adjustments in our garden's repertoire. Water-guzzling plants will lose their cachet and plants that can make it through dry spells will grab our attention. Great consumer education about smart water practices combined with homeowners' voluntary conservation of water indicate a shift in attitudes. "We realize that we can no longer have water on demand," Dr. Mote adds.

▲ ▽ ▲ ▲ ▽ ▲ ▽ ▲ ▽ ▲ ▽ ▲ ▽ ▲ ▽

▲ ▽ ▲ ▲ ▽ ▲ ▽ ▲ ▽ ▲ ▽ ▲ ▽ ▲ ▽

NORTHWEST PRECIPITATION AT A GLANCE

Here's a snapshot of how much or how little precipitation fell on the Northwest in 2003. The figures illustrate some of the obvious differences on either side of the Cascade mountain range. Figures are given in inches.

MONTH	Portland OR	Redmond OR	Seattle WA	Spokane WA
JANUARY	2.46	.94	3.07	.84
FEBRUARY	2.37	.42	1.80	.52
MARCH	5.75	.61	6.49	2.13
APRIL	4.37	.91	2.74	1.41
MAY	1.49	2.18	1.16	1.49
JUNE	.31	.04	.51	.22
JULY	trace	.19	.06	trace
AUGUST	.19	.31	.32	.44
SEPTEMBER	.85	.56	.89	.58
OCTOBER	.51	.25	8.95	.51
NOVEMBER	1.57	.78	6.71	1.57
DECEMBER	2.14	1.69	3.89	2.14

Courtesy AccuWeather.com

To learn more about current precipitation and temperature trends in your region, click on "Gardening" at AccuWeather.com's resource section.

▲ ▽ ▲ ▲ ▽ ▲ ▽ ▲ ▽ ▲ ▽ ▲ ▽ ▲ ▽

Water Wisdom:
Simple Conservation Methods to
Try in Your Garden

The easiest way to determine if water has to be added to the soil is to feel it. If your soil cannot be rolled into a ball, it is probably too dry. If the soil can be molded into a ball that crumbles when you poke it with a finger, it is probably just right. If the molded soil seems like a soggy meatball, it's probably too wet. Sandy soil generally won't form a ball, which is one reason why gardeners with sandy soil conditions add organic compost to improve the soil's integrity.

Use a rain barrel. It's true that the fifty-gallon rain barrels are unlikely to make much impact on lessening your water bill next summer. However, collecting *some* rainwater to use during the dry season is worth trying. You can even place one rain barrel beneath each of several downspouts to "harvest" the abundant rain that comes our way each fall, winter, and spring. Available from many area water utilities, these durable plastic barrels are useful additions to your garden.

Recycle water. Municipalities regulate certain types of household water, such as water from showers, baths, washing machines, and dishwashers—otherwise known as gray water. Even if you wash dishes with environmentally safe soaps, you are restricted from using it to water plants.

Yet you can capture extra water in smaller ways. It's easy to let a pot of water in which you boiled pasta cool, then pour it onto a container plant. When you do this, you've just successfully recycled two gallons of water! While you're waiting for your faucet water to heat up, capture another gallon or so of clean water using a pitcher. The water from a vase of flowers is also easily recycled by pouring it onto a planted container after you've tossed out the arrangement.

Plant like-minded plants together. Group your plants according to their water needs, a strategy that prevents overwatering. That way you're not drenching a drought-tolerant plant growing next to a thirsty one. I like this idea because it forces me to be creative in my garden design choices. For example, when I was in search for a profuse, short plant that could grow at the base of an 'Iceberg' rose hedge, I opted for a hardy geranium rather than lavender. Now established, the roses and *Geranium* 'Johnson's Blue' are suited for each other, preferring a slow, deep watering about twice a month during the summer. The lavender, on the other hand, can survive all summer with little water.

Treat your lawn differently than your borders and beds. Lawns need more water more frequently than most other areas of the garden. One option is to let your lawn go dormant during the summer or grow an eco-lawn blend of plants. If you choose to keep it green, tinker with your watering system so that the lawn-watering schedule is separate from the rest of the garden. Lay out planting areas and irrigation systems to make it easy to water your lawn separately.

Make every drop count. Here are some pointers from the Saving Water Partnership's Smart Watering Guide (see page 121 in "Gardening Resources" for ordering information).

- Choose hose-end sprinklers with spray patterns that match the shape of your lawn or garden.
- Use rotating or oscillating lawn sprinklers, not fixed sprays.
- Minimize evaporation by watering early in the day or late at night, when temperatures are cooler and the wind is calm.
- Place sprinklers where they won't waste water on the driveway, sidewalks, and patios.
- Use timers to limit watering.
- Repair leaky faucets and hoses—even small leaks can be water wasters.
- If you are using an automatic controller–timer, get a rain shut-off detector so you are not irrigating when it is raining.

What makes a plant drought tolerant? Drought tolerance is a concept that varies depending upon where you live. The operative word is "tolerant"; plants can't survive without *any* water, but they tolerate low hydration levels for extended periods of time when the rain clouds dry up. Ornamental grasses, euphorbia varieties, Mediterranean herbs, and even roses can tolerate extended periods of heat and drought. However, *no plant* is drought tolerant from the day it's planted. Most landscapers and garden designers consider a garden to be drought tolerant *once established*. That means you need to consistently water newly planted trees, shrubs, perennials, and ground covers during the first and possibly second growing season. You can begin weaning the plants off such a regular diet of water by the third growing season. Then you'll really see which plants have earned their drought-tolerant reputation.

Watering for All Seasons

Watering for spring planting – The root-ball on a young plant is small and undeveloped. Go ahead and hover. Give your new plant a large, thorough drink. Moisten the surrounding area two to three times the depth and width of the new plant. Pray for rain. Check your plant as often as you want, but don't water until it really needs it. This requires you to hone your observation skills. Gradually apply less water less frequently, perhaps twice a week instead of daily during the first season. When you do water, remember to apply it slowly and deeply—one-half to one hour at a time, depending on how much rain you receive. Your eventual goal is to water one to two times monthly in the heat of summer (80° F and higher). Make sure you sustain this watering schedule until fall rains arrive.

Watering for fall planting – Once you have amended your soil and added fertilizer to the planting hole, place the plant into the hole and fill it with water several times. This technique gives your plant a deep drink of water. Backfill the hole with the remaining soil and add one more final douse of water. It's great to plant during fall, but take note of temperatures. It's probably still warm during the day and not raining enough to provide the plant with its main source of water. Make sure you continue to water fall-planted additions, but only if it appears the plant needs water. When you do water, "Make it a long, slow tall one," jokes Tory Galloway (see below). "The idea is to get those roots reaching for the deep, dark, cool regions of your soil." Rain will eventually take over, usually between November and April. During occasional winter dry spells, remember to check the water needs of any outdoor container plants.

▲ ▼ ▲ ▲ ▼ ▲ ▼ ▲ ▼ ▲ ▼ ▲ ▼ ▲ ▼

DESIGNING A DROUGHT-TOLERANT GARDEN

Tory Galloway, owner of Seattle's Piriformis Nursery, is an expert when it comes to low-maintenance and drought-tolerant plants. She created the specialty nursery after years as a landscaper who received countless requests from clients for plants that could handle the Northwest's dry summers.

In her own east-facing garden in Indianola, on Washington's Kitsap Peninsula, Tory is experimenting with plants that have a Mediterranean flavor and low-water requirements. The garden's sandy soil and the presence of a septic system have guided her choices. Some day, this will be Tory's ultimate retirement garden, but for now, she's only able to visit it on weekends.

"It has been fun to test the toughness of all the low-water plants at Piriformis," Tory says. "We should all congratulate ourselves on reducing our personal demands for water while we increase our personal sense of satisfaction in growing a beautiful garden." For the past two years, the following plants have thrived "searching" for water over her septic system (two-feet-plus down), with no additional summer water. (When gardening above a septic system, you should avoid planting trees. Shrubs, ornamental grasses, and perennials are optimal choices because they have less-aggressive root systems.)

Campanula lactifolia 'Pritchard's Variety' (Pritchard's bellflower) – Blooms in early summer to early autumn; violet-blue flowers. Zones 5–7.

Geranium pratense 'Victor Reiter' (Victor Reiter cranesbill) – Long-lasting blue-purple flowers bloom from summer to early autumn. Zones 4–8.

Hebe x 'Margery Fish' (Margery Fish hebe) – Long-flowering shrub blooms midsummer to early autumn. Zones 8–10.

Hydrangea paniculata 'Pee Wee' (Pee Wee hydrangea) – Blooms late summer to early autumn. Zones 4–8.

Hydrangea quercifolia (oakleaf hydrangea) – White flowers bloom from midsummer to autumn; fabulous bronze foliage in autumn. Zones 5–9.

Rosa x *odorata* 'Mutabilis' (Mutabilis rose or China rose) – Blooms summer to autumn with light-yellow flowers that fade to coppery pink. Zones 6–9.

Tory says you have to harden your heart when tending to a true low-water garden. "Daily or even third-day watering will turn your plant into a water junkie," she warns. "If watering is therapy for you, then plant more containers and leave those tough plants alone."

▲ ▼ ▲ ▲ ▼ ▲ ▼ ▲ ▼ ▲ ▼ ▲ ▼ ▲ ▼

Ideas for a Drought-Tolerant Perennial Garden

A visit to Seattle's Center for Urban Horticulture is a treat, especially if you take in the Soest Herbaceous Display Garden. Created in 1998, the courtyard-style design features eight pie-shaped display beds with 280 species of herbaceous plants that include perennials, annuals, and bulbs. Many of the plants here attract birds, beneficial insects, and butterflies—a delightful bonus in the landscape.

Here are some of the plants featured in two of the display beds.

Bed 1: Partial Shade, Clay-Loam Soil, Limited Irrigation

Bergenia 'Bressingham White' (Bressingham White bergenia) – Pure white flowers bloom mid- to late spring. Zones 4–8.

Bergenia cordifolia 'Perfecta' (Perfecta heart-leaved bergenia) – Pink flowers bloom late winter to early spring. Zones 3–8.

Campanula portenschlagiana (Dalmation bellflower) – Deep purple flowers bloom mid- and late summer. Zones 4–7.

Carex flagellifera (brown sedge) – Brown-tinged grassy foliage is evergreen; flowers are insignificant. Zones 7–9.

Dryopteris filix-mas 'Cristata Martindale'(Cristata Matindale male fern) – Lance-shaped deciduous fern. Zones 4–8.

Hakonechloa macra 'Aureola' (Japanese forest grass or golden Hakone grass) – Bright yellow perennial grass. Zones 5–9.

Helleborus x *sternii* (hellebore) – Creamy green flowers blooming in late winter to mid-spring. Zones 6–9.

Hosta 'Ginko Craig,' (hosta) – Deciduous perennial with summer flowers. Zones 3–8.

Leucanthemum x *superbum* 'Snowcap' and 'Esther Read' (Shasta daisy) – Early summer to early autumn daisylike blooms. Zones 5–8.

Phormium tenax and *Phormium* 'Surfer' (New Zealand flax) – Grown for strong linear (evergreen) foliage rather than flowers. Zones 9–10.

Bed 7: Partial Shade, Sandy-Loam Soil, Limited Irrigation

Athyrium nipponicum 'Pictum' (Japanese painted fern) –
Silvery green and red deciduous fern. Zones 5–8.

Cortaderia selloana 'Pumila'(Pumila pampas grass) –
Produces silvery yellow plumes in late summer. Zones 7–10.

Dryopteris dilatata (broad buckler fern) – Shuttlecock-like
deciduous fern. Zones 5–8.

Erysimum 'Bowles Mauve' (Bowles Mauve wallflower) –
Shrubby evergreen perennial with mauve-colored flowers
in late winter to summer. Zones 6–10.

Euphorbia amygdaloides 'Rubra' (Rubra wood spurge) –
Mid-spring to early summer blooms. Zones 6–9.

E. myrsinites (myrtle spurge) – Succulent blue-gray leaves
with light-green flowers in spring. Zones 5–8.

Gaura lindheimeri (white gaura) – White flowers, late spring
to early autumn bloom. Zones 6–9.

Helleborus foetidus 'Wester Flisk' (Wester Flisk stinking hellebore) – Blooms midwinter to mid-spring. Zones 6–9.

Helleborus orientalis (Lenten rose) – White or greenish cream
flowers bloom midwinter to spring. Zones 4–9.

Miscanthus sinensis 'Gracillimus' (Gracillimus maiden grass) –
Narrow white-ribbed leaves with autumn-blooming panicles.
Zones 4–9.

Origanum vulgare (oregano) – Woody evergreen perennial herb
that flowers midsummer to early autumn. Zones 5–9.

Penstemon 'Hopley's Variegated' (Hopley's Variegated
penstemon) – Lilac-blue flowers bloom midsummer to
mid-autumn. Zones 8–10.

Polystichum munitum (western sword fern) – Leathery
dark-green evergreen fern. Zones 3–8.

Stachys byzantina 'Countess Helen von Stein' (Countess
Helen von Stein lambs' ears) – Velvety gray perennial
with flowers in early summer to autumn. Zones 4–8.

Thalictrum aquilegiifolium (meadow rue) – Fluffy purple-pink
or white flowers in early summer. Zones 5–9.

NATIVE and HABITAT GARDENING

Thanks to the passionate work of local native plant societies, Pacific Northwest gardeners have access to more information about our local flora—and where to find it—than ever before. We've moved beyond the idea that creating a beautiful garden means ripping out all the "weeds" and importing plants straight from Europe's most pristine gardens. Naturalistic gardening is an inspired art form, allowing us to blur the lines between cultivated and uncultivated, responding to the idea of "right plant, right place." Choosing plants already adapted to our soils, temperatures, and climates is one way to eliminate some of the guesswork about which plants will happily exist in our backyards. Moreover, these are the plants that won't need excessive watering, feeding, insecticides, or fungicides in order to look lush, green, and beautiful.

There's another bonus to going native. When you garden with native trees, shrubs, and perennials, you are also providing essential habitats for birds, beneficial insects, and other creatures that are increasingly being displaced due to construction and development.

Thanks to local chapters of native plant groups in Oregon, Washington, and British Columbia, you can access lists of plants uniquely suited to the Northwest's various microclimates. It's fun to attack idiosyncrasies such as wet winters and dry summers or freezing winters and sweltering summers head-on, with plants that actually prefer these conditions. Depending on your location, you can see native plants by visiting public gardens, attending workshops, and scouring the tables at native plant society sales.

Generally, plants that are considered native to the Northwest have survived here for centuries. These plants and their close relatives can be the hardworking stars for your landscape.

Defining Native

Dan Hinkley, the noted horticultural from Heronswood Nursery in Kingston, Washington (on the Olympic Peninsula), began a lecture at the Northwest Flower and Garden Show by projecting an image of Earth onto the big screen. Hinkley used the graphic to remind his audience that he considers any plant that grows on the planet as native. For a person who travels the globe in search of plants in their native habitat, then conducts extensive research and testing in order to bring these specimens to the gardening public, this was a suitable way to start a lecture.

For those of us willing to let him do all that work so we can order the unique and unusual plants from his Web site, it's useful to look at the widely varied definitions of native plants. *Native* is a term most often used to describe plants that grew in the wild before the arrival of European settlers. Yet plants, like people, migrate over time due to climactic and environmental changes, a reality reflected in a broader definition of *native*, describing plants well adapted to our regional conditions that may have become established in the Northwest after it was settled. Another contemporary definition limits the term to plants that originally grew within a fifty-mile radius of a locale prior to the arrival of Europeans.

A visit to the Washington Native Plant Society (WNPS) online (www.wnps.org) will wow you with detailed lists of plants native to specific Washington counties. While that's a pretty narrow definition of what's native, I love the idea of clicking on "Jefferson County," then choosing "Mount Townsend," then reading about no fewer than 238 species (from *Abies amabalis* to *Zigadenus elegans*) of conifers, evergreens, and deciduous trees and shrubs—woody and herbaceous plants that WNPS volunteers have documented along the trails of that one area.

Consider broadening your gardening repertoire to include native plants—it's a great way to better understand our region's unique character. Here are some tips to help you get started, provided by the Oregon Native Plant Society (www.oregonnps.org). The society offers this caveat: Transplanting native plants from a natural habitat to your garden can damage natural plant communities. In addition, state laws nearly always forbid the collection of plant species in the wild without special permits.

Going Native in Your Garden

Use plants that are native to your eco-region. What is an eco-region? Eco-regions are areas that are relatively uniform in soils, vegetation, climate, geology, and wildlife.

Choose plants that grow well in the unique conditions in your garden. The particular conditions of soil type, soil moisture, and amount of sunlight may vary in different parts of your garden. You will want to select the right plants to fit the various conditions that may be present in your garden. For example, if your front yard gets full sun for most of the day, you would want to plant natives from your eco-region that grow in sunny places.

Select plants that originated from as close to your home as possible. Plants that occur in your eco-region and that originate close to your garden site are *locally native*. By using locally native plants, you will preserve the natural heritage of your community. In addition, you will have a higher probability of successfully establishing the plants than if you were to use plants that originated from far away.

Select healthy looking plants. Healthy looking plants exhibit vigorous growth, are not wilted, have good foliage color, and are free of insect damage and spots on the leaves. Healthy nursery plants will have a much better chance of growing well in your garden than unhealthy plants. Once they are established, native plants may attract butterflies and other animals that depend on these plants for their own survival. Welcome these visitors. Attracting these creatures to your garden is one of the many benefits of gardening with natives.

For best results, plant in the spring or fall. At other times of the year, plants will need greater amounts of attention (e.g., watering) in order to flourish.

If you choose to not plant natives, avoid using invasive nonnative plants.

Mimic Nature

Native plant enthusiasts love the way their "local favorites" can bring the woodland, mountains, or shorelines into urban and suburban backyards. One of the ways to make the most of native plants is to mimic how they grow in nature.

Create an appealing plant display by combining native varieties and nonnative ornamentals that respond similarly to moisture and sunlight levels in your own garden. Another way to emulate nature is to plant varying levels of vegetation: canopy (the uppermost layer of vegetation, usually trees), understory (smaller trees and shrubs below the canopy), and ground covers (herbaceous ferns, perennials, and other low-lying plants). Get help in choosing plants to fit your gardening conditions by visiting the Washington State University Master Gardener Web site (http://gardening.wsu.edu) and clicking on the "Native Plant" section. You'll find plants recommendations under such conditions as deep shade/moist soils, partial shade/damp soils, sun/moist soils, and sun/well-drained soils.

I like to seek out native plants that can fill the role of a favorite hybrid or cultivated species. For example, there's something very useful about having common boxwood shrubs (*Buxus sempervirens*, an evergreen species from Europe, Asia, and Central America), because they provide structure, architecture, and can define "rooms" in your garden. At a recent Northwest Flower and Garden Show, I noted that no fewer than five of the showcase garden displays featured a dwarf form of evergreen huckleberries (*Vaccinium ovatum*), a Pacific Northwest native, as hedging. Who needs boxwood when you can have this evergreen, berry-laden option?

Borrowing Natives

Others may choose to broaden the idea of growing locally native plants to growing plants native to an entire region. Plants don't really pay attention to human-imposed city, county, and state borders, so why should gardeners stick to those boundaries when searching for interesting and unique plants?

Whether you're a purist or, like me, prefer to extend the idea of *native* and borrow from adjacent regions or like-minded zones, you can learn a lot by experimenting with plants that border our region. Northern California, for example, offers an exciting lineup of plants that we may be able to grow in some Northwest gardens, giving us a change in plant palette, form, and personality.

When you're borrowing from nearby regions, think about making zone-appropriate choices. Perhaps you live in Zone 7. Some research will show you that places such as New Zealand and Australia, as well as China, Japan, Korea, and parts of Europe, all offer the same zonal profile. If you're in an experimental mood, there are plenty of wonderful plants to seek out and borrow for your own backyard.

Before planting a zone-appropriate plant from another region or country, make sure it is not an invasive species for the Pacific Northwest. I recently stumbled into just such a problem when I listed a plant, grown by a reputable local nursery, in a Northwest Horticulture Society newsletter article. The grower first read about this grasslike annual in a book written by English gardening legend Christopher Lloyd. While Lloyd considered the plant to be a noteworthy addition to a mixed ornamental border, the grower and I soon learned that Washington state included it on a list of noxious weeds.

Landscaping with Natives

The more we learn about native plants, the more appealing they are. Native plants speak to the natural geography of a place, whether they grow in the wild or in our ornamental gardens. In other words, when we integrate native plants into our gardens, we help the landscape fit seamlessly into the region in which we live.

"Gardeners should love native plants," says Carolyn Devine, education director for the Berry Botanic Garden in Portland. "As accent plants, ground covers, and perennials, native plants are adapted to our soils and climate." A visit to the Berry Botanic Garden will introduce you to a broader selection of native plants than you may ever have seen before. They're not all salal shrubs and vine maples. Among other things, including the largest public rock garden on the West Coast, this fabulous public garden is devoted to the conservation of rare and endangered Pacific Northwest plants. You'll learn so much as you stroll the native plant trail complete with interpretive signs that describe how native plants provide habitat for wildlife.

Devine brings us back to the question of how the average gardener defines the term *native*. "It depends on your goals," she says. "For example, in my southeast Portland garden, I aim to provide wildlife habitat and also enjoy growing plants that remind me of the beautiful mountain and coastal landscapes of the Pacific Northwest. To that end, I define *native* to mean a plant that grew, at the time of European settlement, within a seventy-mile radius of my garden." This generous definition allows her to include favorite coastal and subalpine species.

Understandably, that geographic span may not resonate with gardeners who have other goals. She notes, "Those who are particularly knowledgeable and mindful of providing habitat for butterflies may want to have a much narrower definition of natives. Caterpillars can be finicky eaters, so to make sure you provide them the best plant possible you should find native plants that are grown from stock that is as close to your garden as possible."

In general, natives are undemanding garden residents. "For their first few years, native plants still require summer watering," Devine points out. "But once established, they don't mind the wet winters and can survive summer droughts with less water than exotic ornamentals. While all garden plants require some attention to look and perform their best, native plants often require less," she adds.

Anyone who has been seduced by a novel or new perennial that quickly ends up growing—insidiously—in every corner of the garden (and maybe your neighbor's) knows to be careful with self-sowers. While plants from any region have the capacity to become weeds, native plants are not invasive in wild habitats. "They are already established in balanced, local ecosystems so have little or no potential to become invasive pests in our wild and natural areas," Devine explains.

Twice each year, the Berry Botanic Garden offers a "Gardening with Natives" class series. Learn more about this and other programs by calling (503) 636-4112 or visit www.berrybot.org.

Carolyn Devine's
Top Ten Northwest Natives
for the Residential Garden

Arctostaphylos columbiana (hairy manzanita) – This relative of kinnikinnick is one of the best ornamental native plants to be found for year-round interest. You'll love the urn-shaped flowers that bloom late winter to early spring, not to mention its red fruits, silvery evergreen foliage, and wonderful exfoliating bark. Zones 7–10.

Camassia quamash (common camas) – Use this bulb in perennial borders for its stunning blue flowers in spring. Zones 4–10.

Eriophyllum lanatum (Oregon sunshine) – "I am quite fond of this plant because of its cheerful, daisylike blooms that last for much of the summer." An added benefit is that it does not require summer water. Zones 5–8.

Erythronium oregonum (Oregon fawn lily) – While it takes several years for one seedling to bloom, they are well worth the wait. "The mottled leaves and pale-yellow flowers seem timid, but they also signal spring's arrival and a new season of alpine hikes." Zones 3–9.

Fragaria chiloensis (coastal strawberry) – If you need a quick, evergreen ground cover that is relatively easy to remove once you decide what you really want in the space, here's your choice. She cautions, "Only buy one!" The tiny delicious strawberries are an added benefit. "A real winner for wildlife value, it is the larval host plant of several species." White flowers March–August; Zones 7–10.

Polystichum munitum (western sword fern) – The all-purpose plant. "It's hard to kill, transplants well, fills in spaces nicely, and does well in a variety of situations." Evergreen; Zones 3–8.

Ribes sanguineum (red flowering currant) – Hummingbirds love the early spring blooms on this plant. Native to coastal ranges from California to British Columbia, it requires little care and is a beautiful addition to the garden. Zones 6–8.

Symphoricarpos albus (snowberry) – "While some people don't like how this plant can look 'scraggly' in the winter, I admire its white persistent fruits—and the fact that it is a host for several species of checkerspot butterflies." Bell-shaped pink flowers in summer; Zones 3–7.

Vaccinium ovatum (evergreen huckleberry) – This evergreen plant has delicious fruits and urn-shaped flowers that attract hummingbirds. It's also the larval host plant for several species of butterflies. Bears white flowers in late spring to early summer; Zones 7–9.

Viola adunca (western dog violet) – Dark-green, heart-shaped leaves form a lovely ground cover with small lavender-blue flowers with white eyes that bloom in spring. "Butterfly caterpillars eat the leaves of this plant, so if you'd like to see fritillary butterflies in your garden, consider this choice." Zones 4–8.

INVADERS

GARDEN MANAGEMENT STYLE

What's your "garden management style"? Most of us can define our personal approach to the outdoor world by the *degree of control* we want to wield over nature. Are you a dictator, one who won't tolerate a single chomp out of a hosta leaf or a few errant weeds peeking out from between the cobbles? Or are you a laissez-faire gardener, the kind who prefers a hands-off approach that borders on a look of horticultural chaos?

There is plenty of room between these two extremes for all of us. And even those who lean toward the dictator end of the spectrum will find that enjoying a good sense of balance in the garden can be best done by adopting a "live and let live" attitude toward botanical invaders.

In addition to being kinder and gentler to our gardens, we should also be kinder and gentler to ourselves. "We are overstressed and don't want the same pressure in our gardens," said Susan McCoy, president of the Garden Media Group. "There's a strong demand for low-demand gardening that meets low-maintenance lifestyles." In the Garden Media Group's annual report, "What's In What's Out," this trend toward simplification and relaxation is evident. Take note:

▲ ▼ ▲ ▲ ▼ ▲ ▼ ▲ ▼ ▲ ▼ ▲ ▼ ▲ ▼

WHAT'S IN	WHAT'S OUT

Green Revolutions — Chemical Attacks

When we abandon chemicals and start thinking about restoring biological health and balance to our plants and soil, we go a long way toward healing the planet, one garden at a time.

Technorganic Gardening — Pest Destruction

If we can help plants "get off" chemical fertilizers and enable them to grow better in the first place, they'll be healthier and happier.

▲ ▼ ▲ ▲ ▼ ▲ ▼ ▲ ▼ ▲ ▼ ▲ ▼ ▲ ▼

Whether you want a garden that is lush, abundant, and beautiful; undisturbed, serene, and peaceful; or you wish to create a sheltered paradise that attracts wildlife and people in harmony, you can achieve these goals naturally. Letting go and giving up some control is a good place to begin. You may find that a garden democracy is better than a dictatorship.

Organic gardening isn't a dirty phrase that means denying one's garden of its beauty. This philosophy can be achieved with a slight shift in your approach to managing the bugs, weeds, and diseases that inevitably arrive within your garden's boundaries.

WEEDS

A weed is a plant that is not only in the wrong place, but intends to stay.
—Sara Bonnett Stein, *My Weeds*

Perhaps if we could penetrate Nature's secrets, we should find that what we call weeds are more essential to the well-being of the world, than the most precious fruit or grain.
—Nathaniel Hawthorne, *Our Old Home*

Weeds are plants that set up housekeeping in the very spot you don't wish to see them. Like the rampant buttercup that loves my lawn or the red-leafed oxalis that thinks it should be a ground cover beneath the rugosa rose border, weeds are inevitable. Yet something resonates when I read Nathaniel Hawthorne's sentiments. Who knows about the secret life of weeds? I tell myself that they must be of some value to some corner of the earth—even if it doesn't seem to be mine.

What's a Weed?

When considering weeds, I rely on this simple yet useful definition: a weed is *any* undesirable plant that's growing where we wish it wouldn't. Sometimes weeds compete with desirable plants, but usually our objection is aesthetic.

Weeds can

- Be a nuisance
- Be a hazard
- Cause injury to humans and animals (as do poison ivy, poison oak, or poison hemlock)
- Compete with garden plants for soil nutrients, light, and water
- Harbor insect and disease pests

Weeds tend to be very competitive and are capable of taking advantage of disturbed areas. They often produce large amounts of seeds or reproduce quickly. Weeds are generally a problem where the desired crop is doing poorly or the soil is unstable. Not all weeds are bad; indeed there are some "good" weeds. Although white clover is often considered a weed in lawns, its benefits may outweigh its negatives. White clover stays green when your lawn goes dormant. In addition, its roots support bacteria that transform nitrogen from the air into plant fertilizer, so clover actually feeds the lawn.

Invasive Weeds and How to Outsmart Them

I've always been in awe of fellow gardeners who can instantly rattle off the names and growth habits of the typical Northwest weeds. A group of volunteers at the Master Gardener Urban Demonstration Garden in Bellevue planted a "common weed display garden." So, if someone comes in with a weed question, the clinic volunteers have something against which to compare the person's sample.

Even without memorizing all the names of weeds, I've finally accepted that life in the garden is easier if I familiarize myself with types of weeds and the way they grow. You can classify weeds by *appearance* or *life cycle*. Here are some useful guidelines.

Appearance

Broad-leaves – Broad-leaf weeds generally have tap-roots (such as a dandelion) or fibrous roots (such as lamb's-quarters). These plants are also called dicots, with veins that radiate from a single larger vein.

Grasses – Also called monocots, grassy weeds have long, narrow leaves with veins that are parallel to each other. Grasses have fibrous root systems.

Life Cycle

Annual weeds – Annual weeds germinate, grow, flower, and set seed in one year or less, just like their ornamental and edible annual counterparts. Temperature, light, and moisture trigger germination. Annual weeds spread only by seed. Examples include mustards and chickweed, both of which germinate in late summer or fall, overwinter, and then flower the following spring. Redroot pigweed and lamb's-quarters germinate in late spring, grow during the heat of summer, flower, set seed, and die from cold temperatures. You can control the spread of most annual weeds by removing them before they set seed.

Biennial weeds – Biennial plants, such as bull thistle and garlic mustard, complete their life cycle in two growing seasons. They germinate and form a rosette—a dense whorl of leaves arising from the central point of the plant—the first year. During the second growing season, biennials grow a stem, flower, set seed, and die. You can control them by hoeing or digging when they are small.

Perennial weeds – Perennial plants can grow for many years. Dandelions and other simple perennials spread only by seed. (Remember all those fluffy seed heads you blew on as a kid? Now that you are a gardener, you may rue your past deeds. Mother Nature has come back to haunt you.)

Some perennials multiply by seed or by underground reproductive structures. Quack grass spreads by rhizomes (underground, horizontal stems). Canada thistle and field bindweed have a spreading root system. Other perennial weeds, such as yellow nutsedge, have small tubers. Control of perennial weeds is difficult because of their extensive underground root systems. Removal efforts pay off if you are persistent, but you have to eradicate all of the root material or the perennial weed will return, sometimes with a greater vengeance since what was once root has been broken into bits, each of which sprouts a new plant.

WEED CONTROL

- **Eliminate weeds early in the growing season, before they have a chance to develop roots or set seeds.**
- **Prevent weeds from entering the garden. Deadhead the seed heads of any neighborhood weeds you notice (in my neighborhood, it's the crop of wild geranium plants that grows on the median running the length of our steep street). Don't use fresh manure. Keep an eye on weeds that arrive in the base of nursery pots. For example, when I brought home a hardy succulent from a nonprofit gardening organization's plant sale, I received some surprise "freebies"—in the form of a few knotweed seedlings. While the prices and selections at this "grassroots" sale were enticing, many of the plant choices came from the group's member gardens—and unfortunately, so did the weeds!**
- **Cultivate on a sunny, warm day, so weeds you've pulled or tilled will dry out and die.**
- **Apply at least two and up to six inches of mulch, depending on the soil and surrounding plantings, to prevent weed seedlings from emerging.**
- **Remove weed clippings from your garden if there is a chance seeds have already set. Do not put them on the compost pile.**

Prevention, or Nip It in the Bud

Proactive gardeners do what they can to prevent weeds from ever becoming established in the garden. If you only purchase well-rotted animal manure, you can avoid errant weed seeds from establishing themselves in your ornamental beds. If you give or receive perennial plant divisions, make sure you've removed any weed seedlings from the pot. And keep an eye on weeds bordering the garden from going to seed. If that means offering to help your neighbor with weed control, by all means do!

Mechanical Control

Good, old-fashioned weeding is the most common way to eradicate weeds. The methods vary but each requires sweat equity to clear out the invaders: hand-pulling, hoeing, tilling, or digging out underground portions of weeds takes time and energy, but is usually very effective. I subscribe to the "see it, take immediate action" school of thought, comparable to cleaning up the kids' piles of junk around the house. If you can dig out a nasty weed the minute it catches your attention, you will gradually win the battle. Also, you won't be as exhausted as you would be if you save all the weeding for the week before your garden party.

Cultural Control

Employing cultural weed-fighting controls allows a gardener to observe the overall environment of the garden and decide whether nonchemical methods and techniques will work. Most of the ideas below are not foolproof; however, they're designed to smother or weaken weeds.

Competitive crops – I liken this to "displacement theory" gardening. All plants in the garden compete for light, water, and nutrients. Lawn (turf), ground covers, and some edible crops, such as potatoes, can compete well with weeds because of their quick growth and dense foliage. Planting evergreen ground covers is extremely satisfying because their presence is both aesthetically pleasing and a foil for emerging weeds.

Mowing – Clipping weeds slows their growth, preventing weed plants from going to seed. Use a lawn mower, clippers, or other tools to cut back weeds before they have a chance to spread, reproduce, or set seed. Mowing will not eliminate perennial weeds, but at least it can control their spread to some degree.

Mulching – Mulching is the practice of covering soil with a material that prevents light from reaching the seeds and smothers any seeds that may germinate. Straw, sawdust, compost, pine straw, or grass clippings (apply clippings only one-half inch at a time if fresh) are organic choices. I've even had success with thick layers of wet newspaper or cardboard, over which I layer compost. If weeds are able to penetrate the mulch layer, it's relatively easy to pull out their seedlings. By spreading at least two inches of organic mulch, you'll help the soil warm up faster as well as retain moisture. One caveat: if there is any latent rootstock from perennial weeds in your soil (such as thistle or horsetail), mulching will do little to suppress spreading. That's when you return to the mechanical controls such as hand weeding.

Cover crops – Consider a cover crop to choke out many germinating weeds. You can use a summer cover, such as buckwheat, or a winter cover, such as oats, barley, or rye. Till the cover crop into the soil before it flowers and it will add beneficial nutrients to the soil as it breaks down.

Least Toxic Controls

Herbicides with low toxicity to beneficial garden life, people, and wildlife are worth trying before you resort to synthetic products.

Corn gluten – A milling by-product that is used as animal feed, corn gluten prevents the growth of weed seedlings and actually fertilizes established plants. It is sold under several brand names. Its effect is short-lived, so applications must be timed to coincide with weed germination. It is often used as a preemergent for lawn weeds.

Herbicidal soaps and vinegar – Both of these damage leaf cells and dry out plants. Tough weeds resist these herbicides or resprout from roots. Use concentrated vinegar products carefully; be sure to use protective eyewear.

Chemical Control

This is the method of last resort, as herbicides that kill weeds are indeed chemicals. Consider the disadvantages of using herbicides:

- They are difficult to apply accurately. When you spray or spread them, you run the risk of the weed-killer damaging other plants in the garden.
- Proper storage and handling may be a problem, especially if you have children or pets.
- Many herbicides are plant- or crop-specific, thus you run the risk of using them incorrectly.

The only chemical weed control that I feel comfortable recommending is concentrated Roundup, which I apply directly to the weed. Roundup works well in fighting recurring weeds in walkways, where you know spraying will hit only the dandelion rather than nearby ornamental plants. You can also spot-kill weeds growing among other good plants by painting the leaves and stems with Roundup without risk to the valuable ornamentals nearby.

Quick Guide to Weeds

The list offered here is an introduction to some of the most troublesome, invasive, and noxious weeds in our region. There are many more.

To identify a weed in your garden, check the "Gardening Resources" section for good information on regional guides, plus some useful Web sites with photographs and plant fact-sheets. In addition, many hours of training, as well as personal experience, have prepared your local Master Gardener diagnostic clinic to help identify and tackle invasive weeds. You can always take a sample of a problematic weed to a clinic where you'll receive identification help and useful advice on weed removal.

Worst Weeds Pervasive in Northwest Gardens

Blackberries – Urban, suburban, and rural gardeners can't seem to eradicate blackberries once they take over an abandoned or neglected area of the garden. An entire blackberry removal industry is supported by the output of this aggressively spreading vine that crushes anything in its path.

Burdock – A coarse, extensively branched, biennial herb, burdock's broad heart-shaped leaves can't be missed when they appear in your lawn. In its second year the plant produces a two- to four-foot stem with numerous heads of lavender-purple flowers. Because its young leaves can be prepared like spinach, burdock is thought to have first arrived in North America as a vegetable.

Buttercup – Anyone with wet, clay soil knows this persistent weed, often called creeping buttercup. It spreads effectively and rapidly as its prostrate stems root at the nodes, imbedding themselves in your lawn, pathways, and border edges. Many weekends have been spent digging deep into the dirt, trying to pull up this tenacious weed with tiny yellow buttercup flowers and shiny green, lobed leaves.

Garlic mustard – Unlike many problem weeds, garlic mustard is shade tolerant and can successfully invade forest habitats. It usually gains access through disturbed areas, such as stream banks disturbed by flooding, roadsides, trails, or campgrounds. Garlic mustard produces large numbers of seeds and is self-pollinating, which allows a single plant to quickly produce enough offspring to dominate a site.

Horsetail – Distinguished by their succulent, hollow, jointed stems and bottlebrush foliage, horsetails are widely distributed throughout North America. The Northwest has not avoided this nuisance; horsetails populate moist fields and gardens. Giant horseail can exceed six feet in height, so try hiding it with dense plantings of taller shrubs. Also called scouring rush, it was used historically for cleaning pots and pans.

English ivy – When English ivy spreads, it transforms into a botanical monster, overtaking shaded, forested lands and natural areas such as parks. There's an aggressive movement to eradicate ivy from our region—with vine removal efforts concentrated everywhere from forested areas to city parks containing old-growth trees.

When we moved to our Seward Park home in south Seattle, my family inherited ivy that had been intentionally planted—probably forty years ago—along the rockery that borders the north and south sides of our property. We can't rip it out completely without destroying the vintage stone retaining walls. It has been an ongoing battle keeping the vines from creeping into the rest of the garden. I cut it back to the base of the wall each quarter, filling huge yard-waste bags with the vines.

Knapweeds – Members of the sunflower family, knapweeds have knoblike flowering heads with tubular disc flowers. Russian knapweed, Montana knapweed, and even blue cornflower, or bachelor's buttons, are among the familiar annual invaders in this group.

Nightshade – Part of the potato family, bittersweet nightshade has a woody base and grows from rhizomes. Its vinelike stems spread over the ground and other vegetation. Flowers resemble those of a tomato plant, with five-pointed petals.

Tansy – Tansy ragwort and common tansy are not related, but they are like-minded weeds. Tansy ragwort, a short-lived but aggressive perennial weed that's poisonous to livestock, grows from a taproot to about three feet. Its golden flowers resemble tiny dandelions; the foliage resembles carrot leaves. Common tansy is a perennial weed that spreads by rhizomes.

Thistles – Thistles are also in the sunflower family. The numerous varieties are distinguished by their spiny bracts, leaves, and stems. Despite their attractive heads and nectar for bees and butterflies, these coarse biennials are prolific seed producers. Seeds ride the wind, finding their way to gardens, roadsides, and fields. One way to control thistles is to cut the flowering stem to the ground after it sprouts.

Other Thoughts on Weeds

Nature Abhors a Monoculture

Mix it up. Sometimes the best thing we can do about a patch of unrelenting weeds is to search for an ornamental plant that might outsmart it. I'm thinking about a few invaders in my own garden, such as the ever-present buttercup that persistently reappears even after aggressive weeding sessions. Luckily, a friend has shared a flat of his cherished ground cover called *Waldsteinia ternata*, a semi-evergreen perennial with dark-green toothed foliage and bright-yellow saucer-shaped flowers (in fact, it kind of looks like an upscale version of buttercup). This lovely spreader likes my shaded border and appears to be crowding out (or at least hiding evidence of) its weedy look-alike.

Similarly, I've been able to mask weeds that grow beneath a hedge of 'Iceberg' roses by planting a hardy geranium on either side of each rose. They're long-blooming, casual spreaders that hide almost any weed that dares to grow beneath them. Moreover, in Seattle, the geranium foliage usually looks great even in the winter. I've finally found a few stars that can hide unwanted weeds and look attractive at the same time.

Displacement Theory

Weeds seem to love bare soil as much as they love disturbed soil. Of course, these facts offer a plant-junkie like me the best excuse for *buying and growing more plants.* Yet growing anything attractive is more appealing than looking at weeds, so I'm a big advocate for ground covers, which can help carpet the soil area below shrubs, trees, and taller perennials.

Out of Control

We're all aware of noxious weeds—those the state, county, and municipal weed police have targeted for removal. However, some of our most challenging weeds are ornamental plants that don't know when to quit. I chuckled when plant explorer Dan Hinkley recently described *Euphorbia dulcis* 'Chameleon' (a beautiful black-purple addition to the garden that vigorously sows itself) as follows: "We no longer send it to you by UPS. We just give it your address and it will find you." When it comes to running trials of potentially aggressive ornamental plants, Hinkley and the Heronswood Nursery staff are some of the most responsible folks around. If a plant seems to be invasive or too eager to spread, they don't sell it.

Some of us have a low tolerance level for plants that tend to creep beyond the hole in which we first planted them. I recently visited a gorgeous formal garden in Seattle's Queen Anne neighborhood. The homeowner lamented that hired help now spend all their time removing Japanese anemone from the white border. She obviously has a lower tolerance for this plant than do I. While Japanese anemone tends to spread a little too exuberantly, I consider that a trade-off for the gift of prolific late-summer flowers on stems that tower above everything else. And in reality, Japanese anemone seedlings aren't that hard to pull out by hand.

Good garden stewardship requires us to be aware of the potential for "out of control" ornamental plants that spread too aggressively. We should enjoy our gardens, while keeping an eye out for problem plants that could invade others'.

PESTS
LARGE and SMALL

In the hierarchy of life, I fear weeds more than I do garden pests. Nevertheless, every garden is different. I know my little world is vastly different from those of gardening friends just fifteen miles east of Seattle, in the foothills of the Cascades. That's where people worry about larger garden invaders, such as deer, moles, and other herbivores in search of food.

There's a big difference between noticing that your roses have been nibbled to the nub and observing a few tiny slug bites out of the hostas. You can learn a lot about the health of your garden by observing the insect activity. A healthy landscape is one that keeps most insect pests in check by natural forces.

Who's Eating My Garden?

Pests – A pest can be an insect, animal, plant, or microorganism that causes problems in the garden. This broader definition helps us differentiate between problem insects and beneficial insects.

Beneficials – Beneficials are organisms in the air, on the ground, or in the soil that do good things for your garden. When it comes to insects, most are valuable garden residents. Beneficial insects will eat the pests that harm your plants, pollinate fruit trees and berries, eat plant waste and break it down, aerate and improve the soil, as well as provide food for birds and animals that also eat pests.

Beneficial pests – Some pests are also beneficials. Yellow jackets, for example, are predators of pests. However, they can also be painful to humans in the garden.

It's important to be informed about the creatures that are

dining on your beautiful plants, otherwise you might be killing beneficial insects that your garden desperately needs. Can you let nature manage pest and disease control? English horticulturist Timothy Walker of the Oxford University Botanic Garden in Oxford, England, said he was giving up on fighting slugs in the hosta border: "We'd been spraying the plants for more than 300 years and it still hadn't worked," he confided. When you pay attention to cultural conditions, you vastly improve the garden's chances of enduring periodic attacks by both bugs and disease. Healthy soil, good drainage, and smart plant placement (natives and exotics that enjoy similar conditions grown together) are all ways to improve a land-scape's ability to stay healthy.

If you can accept minor damage to your plants, you will actually have a healthier garden than one in which there are no bites, tears, or holes. It's not realistic to expect a totally pest-free garden. Fortunately, many healthy plants maintain their own resources to endure or outgrow the disease or insect that affects them. If you are willing to leave pest control to the "good bugs," you'll soon see nature at work.

▲ ▼ ▲ ▲ ▼ ▲ ▼ ▲ ▼ ▲ ▼ ▲ ▼ ▲ ▼

ATTRACTING GOOD BUGS

When you grow a variety of plants that provide nectar and pollen, you'll encourage a diversity of beneficial bugs to reside in your garden. This method of gardening will attract "good bugs" and give them something to eat while they wait around for the pests to arrive or hatch. Birds are also natural predators of invasive insects, so encourage their presence in your garden by growing trees for shelter and shrubs for berries. Provide a good source of water as well.

▲ ▼ ▲ ▲ ▼ ▲ ▼ ▲ ▼ ▲ ▼ ▲ ▼ ▲ ▼

▲ ▼ ▲ ▲ ▼ ▲ ▼ ▲ ▼ ▲ ▼ ▲ ▼ ▲ ▼

PREVENTIVE MEDICINE

As horticulture instructor and coordinator of the South Seattle Community College's (SSCC) Arboretum, Van Bobbitt is a seasoned veteran when it comes to landscape management. However, while some think the secret to having a green garden (where all the plants have great-looking foliage, bark, and blooms) is eradicating garden pests, he takes a different approach. Bobbitt explains of his holistic approach to landscape management, "I like to focus on plant health rather than pest management."

Van Bobbitt's Garden Practical Philosophy

Know your plants. Conduct an inventory of your entire garden to familiarize yourself with what's growing there. "Know what culture each plant prefers," Bobbitt points out. "Does it like wet or dry soils, sun or shade?"

Know potential problems. With each region, there are some key disease- or pest-prone plants. Sometimes it's futile to try to grow them successfully, but don't despair. You have thousands of other great options to plant. For example, Master Gardeners see more rhododendron, dogwood, spruce, rose, and azalea problems than problems with other plants. Ironically, these are some of the Pacific Northwest's basic garden plants. "If you know that 'Port Orford' cedar is prone to root rot, you might want to avoid planting it," Bobbitt cautions.

Rethink your landscape. If you begin viewing your garden as an ecosystem, you'll notice its unique microclimates. "This mind-set enhances plant health care," Bobbitt advocates. "You'll start grouping all your drought-tolerant plants, so you're not watering to the lowest common denominator." You'll choose the more disease-resistant cultivar of a favorite plant genus. You'll begin understanding drainage patterns, the length of sun your garden receives in each area and prevailing winds.

Take note. You can practice both the art and science of gardening, noticing the dynamic changes that occur with the seasons. Notice if a plant seems particularly stressed (yellow or wilted leaves, dead twigs, etc.) and keep an eye out for potential pest problems. Make sure to monitor your plants that have the most potential for susceptibility to pests and diseases.

Fight back. Remember, chemical use should be your last resort. You may have several other choices, including leaving well enough alone. Bobbitt elucidates: "No action can be a valid approach—it gets back to your threshold level. For home gardeners, it's usually an aesthetic threshold. What level of disease or pests can you tolerate? The more you know about what is entailed to keep your garden looking 'perfect,' the more imperfection you might be willing to tolerate."

Chemicals are not a magic bullet to eradicate all diseases or bugs from the garden. Be sure you are well informed about the specific purpose of an insecticide or fungicide before you use it.

Practice moderation. Bobbitt uses an analogy between human health and plant health: "If we humans just sit around eating rich food, is that healthy? Or are we healthier eating a moderate diet and exercising?"

"Likewise, garden plants that experience moderate stress often seem better able to withstand pests and diseases that those that have been pampered with excess water or feeding," Bobbitt concludes. "Too much water and fertilizer promote excessive growth, often at the expense of carbohydrate storage, production of defensive chemicals, and root growth—things that help plants better withstand pests, diseases, and serious environmental stresses. Plants on a lean diet of water and nutrients are generally stronger and live longer."

▲ ▼ ▲ ▲ ▼ ▲ ▼ ▲ ▼ ▲ ▼ ▲ ▼ ▲ ▼

Plants That Attract Beneficials

Achillea spp. (yarrow) – Early summer blooms; Zones 4–8.

Anethum graveolens (dill) – Summer blooms; Zones 8–10.

Angelica spp. (angelica) – Late summer flower heads; Zones 5–8.

Anthriscus cerefolium (common chervil) – Blooms midsummer; Zones 7–10.

Calendula officinalis (calendula or pot marigold) – Blooms spring to autumn; Zones 6–10.

Ceanothus spp. (ceanothus or California lilac) – Spring to early summer bloom; Zones 7–10.

Centranthus ruber (red valerian) – Late spring to late summer bloom; Zones 6–10.

Coriandrum sativum (cilantro) – Summer flowers; Zones 6–9.

Erigeron spp. (Santa Barbara daisy) – Spring to autumn bloom; Zones 6–10.

Foeniculum vulgare (fennel) – Summer flowers; Zones 5–10.

Helianthus annuus (sunflower) – Blooms in late summer; Zones 4–10.

Iberis sempervirens (candytuft) – Blooms spring to summer; Zones 7–10.

Leucanthemum spp. (Shasta daisy) – Mid- to late summer flowers; Zones 5–8.

Levisticum officinale (lovage) – Summer flowers; Zones 3–10.

Lobularia maritima (sweet alyssum) – Summer bloom; Zones 7–10.

Monarda didyma (bee balm) – Flowers in summer; Zones 4–9.

Myrrhis odorata (sweet cicely) – Summer flowers; Zones 5–10.

Petroselinum crispum (parsley) – Zones 7–9.

Ruta graveolens (rue) – Summer flowers; Zones 5–9.

Solidago spp. (goldenrod) – Blooms late summer to early autumn; Zones 4–9.

Symphoricarpos albus. (snowberry) – Spring bloom; Zones 3–9.

Thymus spp. (thyme) – Summer bloom; Zones 7–10.

Trifolium spp. (clover) – Summer bloom; Zones 7–10.

Good Bugs:
Ten Top Beneficials for Your Garden

Ladybug – Most people know what an adult ladybug, or lady beetle, looks like, but the larvae are more valuable. They are soft bodied and alligator shaped with black and orange markings. The adults and larvae feed on aphids, mealybugs, scale insects, spider mites, and many insect eggs. Grow flowers that produce pollen and nectar such as dill and angelica to attract ladybugs.

Ground beetle – Ground beetles vary in appearance, but are usually a shiny black, sometimes with a metallic sheen. Some look ferocious, but they are not known to bite people. Adult beetles range from one-eighth to one inch long. They feed on many soil-inhabiting pests such as cutworms and root maggots. Some eat slugs and snails.

Rove beetle – When it holds the tip of its abdomen up in the air, a rove beetle resembles a tiny scorpion. They are fast moving and measure one-tenth to one inch long. The rove beetle eats aphids, springtails, mites, nematodes, slugs, snails, fly eggs, and maggots. They also eat and help break down decaying organic material.

Soldier beetle – A distinctive black abdomen and bright red head or thorax distinguishes the adult soldier beetle. Approximately one-half inch long, this beneficial preys upon aphids, caterpillars, grasshopper eggs, and beetle larvae. Some are attracted to flowering nectar sources.

Assassin bug – This vicious-looking bug is about one-fourth to one inch long, with a cone-shaped head and wide curving beak. It can cause a harmful bite to humans if captured (some species squeak if caught). The adult and nymph assassin bugs use their beaks to stab their prey. They feed on flies, mosquitoes, beetles, and large caterpillars.

Green lacewing – Adult green lacewings have delicate light-green bodies, large clear wings, and bright golden- or copper-colored eyes. They are one-half to three-fourths inch long. The larvae are small, grayish brown, and narrow, with pincerlike mandibles. Eggs are found on plant stems and foliage; they are laid singly or in small groups. Both adults and larvae feed on aphids, insect eggs, and spider mites.

Tachnid fly – Resembling a housefly, a tachnid fly ranges from one-third to one-half inch in length and may be brown, gray, or black in color. Many are parasites of pest caterpillars including cutworms, codling moths, tent caterpillars, cabbage loopers, and gypsy moth larvae. Adults feed on nectar, so include flowers and herbs in the Umbelliferae family in your garden, such as dill, parsley, and Queen Anne's lace, to attract them.

Hoverfly – The adults have bodies with black and yellow stripes. While they may look like bees or wasps, they don't sting. Both adults and larvae are about one-half inch long. Many hoverfly larvae prey on aphids, mealybugs, and other small insects. Adult hoverflies are great garden pollinators.

Dragonfly and damselfly – There are nearly eighty species in Washington, most of which are identified by their long, narrow bodies, large compound eyes, and four transparent wings. These delicate flies are reliable predators of mosquitoes, aphids, and other pests. They are usually attracted to water in the garden, such as a pond.

Bees, wasps, and hornets – Mason bees, honeybees, and bumblebees are desired guests in any garden, especially for their pollinating skills. Different species of wasps attack aphids, whiteflies, and moths. Hornets eat many pests, including crane flies.

Managing Your Garden Naturally

Tips to Get You Started on Managing Your Garden Naturally

Create a healthy garden to stop pest problems before they start. Healthy plants and soil not only resist pests and diseases, they also encourage beneficial garden life.

Identify pests before you spray, stomp, or squash. When you see damaged plants, first identify the suspects. What you think is a bad bug could actually be a friend to the garden. Check the sources cited on page 121 in the "Gardening Resources" section to learn about typical garden pests and beneficials.

Give nature a chance to work. Do not try to eliminate pests at the first sign of damage. Many pests are food for beneficial insect populations. If you remove them, you could be hurting the good bugs in your garden.

Use the least-toxic pest controls available. You can often control pests by using traps or barriers, or by simply removing them (along with an infested branch or stem). These methods don't harm beneficial garden life or the environment. If pesticides seem like your only option for pest control, choose the least-toxic products and follow the tips listed below.

Prevention

The ideas outlined here are provided courtesy of the Natural Lawn and Garden program of the Saving Water Partnership (a coalition of water utilities in the Seattle–King Counties region). You'll notice that the safe bug-control practices are very similar to safe weed-control practices covered on pages 76–81. It all adds up to the importance of maintaining a responsible and respectful attitude toward our environment.

Follow these proactive steps to achieve a healthier garden.

Build healthy soil to grow healthy plants. Amend and mulch entire growing beds with compost. Feed the area *moderately* with organic or slow-release fertilizers, which will enable you to grow vigorous, pest-resistant plants.

Plant right. Place each plant in the light and soil conditions it prefers. Select varieties that are known to grow well under your garden's conditions. Seek out plants that resist common pest and disease problems.

Give your plants space. Good air circulation can prevent or reduce many diseases and pest problems. When you space plants so they have plenty of room to grow, you ensure that plants aren't susceptible to fungal or bacterial attacks, or weakened by pest attacks. Take note: This point often seems directly contradictory to a favorite weed-prevention technique of growing plants so closely together that they crowd out unwanted weeds. You can strike a balance between these two seemingly opposite gardening tips, depending on the plants you are growing.

Clean up. Remove weeds, wood boards, and other yard debris that can harbor pests and diseases. Fruit and fallen leaves from plants such as apple trees and roses with persistent diseases such as scab, rust, and mildew should be put in curbside yard-waste containers. Do not toss them on your home compost pile or dump them into a ravine.

Diversify and rotate annual crops. Grow a variety of plants to prevent problems from spreading, as well as to attract pest-eating insects and birds. Do not plant the same type of annual vegetable in the same spot each year. By rotating the tomato bed or the pea patch, you'll help prevent diseases and pests from building up in the soil.

Pest Controls

Several regions throughout the Northwest have been pre-occupied with recent summer tent caterpillar invasions. While the pests created an unsightly mess of sticky tentlike webs along tree branches, and while many trees suffered defoliation, the overall problem was more aesthetic than harmful. Yet the attack prompted many to hire pest-control companies to spray insecticides on the trees. The periodic arrival of tent caterpillars may just be Mother Nature's way of controlling the environment. By the time the pest-control trucks arrived with spray guns, natural predators had begun to discover and attack the tent caterpillars, and thus nature could have been allowed to take its course. Many pest-control experts say it's unlikely we'll see an aggressive infestation of tent caterpillars in the near future.

If you're worried about a bug infestation in your garden, try these nontoxic methods of control. Physical, rather than chemical controls are the first recommended line of attack because they have no harmful affect on other garden bugs, plants, people, or the environment.

Removal – Pests and diseased plant parts can be picked or washed off plants to control infestations. Just as you pull weeds, you can pick bugs and remove damaged foliage.

Handpicking – Handpicking can be effective for larger pests, such as cabbage loopers, tomato hornworms, slugs, and snails.

Pruning and plucking – Pruning out infestations of tent caterpillars is effective on a small scale. Plucking of infested sections of leaf crops may help remove leaf miners. Be sure to dispose of infested material in curbside yard-waste collection containers rather than in your compost pile.

Washing – Washing aphids from plants with a strong jet spray of water from a hose can reduce the damage these pests cause, especially if you catch them early. Repeated washings may be required before you get the upper hand.

Traps – It's possible to maintain control over pests such as moths and slugs by trapping them. At the very least, these methods help reveal the extent of your pest population.

- **CODLING MOTH TRAPS** Orchard owners use cardboard or burlap wrapped around apple tree trunks in summer and fall to combat codling moth larvae. The material fools the larvae into thinking they have found a safe place to spin their cocoons as they crawl down the tree. You can peel the traps away periodically to remove cocoons.

- **SLUG TRAPS** You can drown slugs in a shallow tray filled with beer. A recycled margarine tub or the type of saucer that fits under a potted plant is ideal. If you don't want to have saucers of beer sitting around your garden, mix up a batch of yeast water by stirring the contents of a single-size packet of yeast into one cup of water. Be sure to dump out dead slugs and frequently replenish the liquid.

Barriers – Physically protect certain plants from pests by using simple barriers.

- **FLOATING ROW COVERS** Floating row covers are lightweight fabrics (often polyspun, such as Reemay) that let light, air, and water reach plants while keeping pests away. Placed over the plants early enough in the season, they are useful for fighting infestations of rust flies on carrots, leaf miners on spinach, and root maggots on cabbage, broccoli, and cauliflower. For plants that require pollinators, remove the row covers when bloom begins.

- **NETTING MESH** Netting keeps birds away from berries and small fruit trees.

- **TANGLEFOOT OR STICKY TAPE** A band of sticky material around tree trunks stops ants from climbing trees and introducing disease-carrying aphids. It can also catch caterpillars that may crawl up the tree to feed at night and down to rest in the daytime.

▲ ▼ ▲ ▲ ▼ ▲ ▼ ▲ ▼ ▲ ▼ ▲ ▼ ▲ ▼

SLUGS 101

Northwest gardeners blame slugs for many of their garden woes. These slimy pests love wet, moist conditions and tasty, lush, green foliage. If you have trouble with slugs, follow these tips. Use chemicals as the last resort … or just learn to live with the critters.

Reduce slug habitat. Keep your garden clean and free of debris, since slugs like to hide under objects that provide dark, wet conditions. Once you weed or prune, dispose of the waste promptly. Avoid heavy ground covers or mulches near plants that are most susceptible to slugs.

Grow plants slugs don't like. Over time, observe which plants slugs prefer and which ones they seem to ignore.

Remove and destroy slugs when you see them. A good evening garden activity, you can find and remove active slugs with a flashlight in one hand and a glove on the other. Drop them into a jar of soapy water to ensure immediate death.

Go for the eggs. During the fall you will find masses of eggs. Stomp or crush them to eliminate hundreds of future slugs in just seconds.

Use barriers. Copper barriers are most effective around susceptible plants and can be attached to raised beds or containers to control slug attacks. Gardeners have also reported success using pea gravel, ground oyster shells, diatomaceous earth, eggshells, and other sharp material as barriers.

Bait stations. If you must use a chemical product, use it carefully and in a secure location to protect children, pets, and birds.

▲ ▼ ▲ ▲ ▼ ▲ ▼ ▲ ▼ ▲ ▼ ▲ ▼ ▲ ▼

Choosing Pesticides

If physical pest controls don't seem to work, you may need to consider pesticides. Use these products and methods with a good dose of caution. Even through they have a low toxicity or break down quickly into safe by-products when exposed to sunlight or soil, they can be toxic to beneficial garden life, people, pets, and other animals. If your garden is above or upstream from lakes, rivers, streams, or other large bodies of water, you may be unintentionally poisoning fish and other water creatures.

Soaps, Oils, and Minerals

Horticultural oil – Horticultural oil smothers mites, aphids and their eggs, scale, leaf miners, mealybugs, and many other garden pests. It comes in varying "weights" for the different seasons. These products have little effect on most beneficials.

Horticultural soap – Also known as insecticidal soap, horticultural soap dries out aphids, whiteflies, earwigs, and other soft-bodied insects. It must be sprayed directly onto the pests to work, so repeated applications may be necessary. There are also soap-based fungicides and herbicides worth trying before using chemical-based products.

Sulfur – Sulfur is an old-time, respected fungicide still used today. It controls many fungal diseases, such as scab, rust, leaf curl, and powdery mildew, without harming most animals and beneficials. For greater effectiveness, sulfur can be mixed with lime. Sulfur is also frequently combined with other materials to create fungicides that are more toxic.

Baking soda solution – A mixture of one teaspoon of baking soda, several drops of Ivory Liquid, and one quart of water can be used on roses to prevent mildew. The solution keeps well for several months. It also works for black spot on roses and powdery mildew on zinnias and other mildew-prone plants.

Slug bait – Iron phosphate slug baits are less toxic than other slug baits and not as hazardous to dogs.

Tip **Never spray any product when the temperature is over 80° F or on a windy day. Be sure to coat the tops and bottoms of the plants' leaves and stems. Always follow manufacturer's instructions. Wear a mask and eye protection whenever spraying.**

Botanicals

Plant-derived insecticides degrade relatively quickly when exposed to sunlight or soil. However, most are initially toxic to people, animals, fish, and other beneficials in the garden. Use with caution and follow label instructions closely, just as if you were using chemical pesticides.

Neem – Neem oil, derived from the neem tree, a native of India, kills and disrupts feeding and mating of many insects, including some beneficials. Also effective as a fungicide, neem oil is the least-toxic botanical.

Biocontrols

Bacillus thuringiensis – Most commonly know as Bt, *Bacillus thuringiensis* is a common, commercially available bacterium that poisons caterpillar pests, including cutworms, armyworms, tent caterpillars, cabbage loopers, and corn earworms. Bt is not toxic to people, animals, fish, and insects—although it *can kill* caterpillars of nonpest butterflies and moths. It must be applied when the caterpillar is small—usually less than one-half inch long, or it will not be effective.

Nematodes – Predatory nematodes kill a wide variety of pests including cutworms, armyworms, root maggots, crane fly larvae, root weevil larvae, and other soil-dwelling pests. Proper soil temperature and moisture are required for nematodes to be effective. You can purchase boxes of live nematodes at specialty nurseries.

Beauveria bassiana – *Beauveria bassiana* is a commercially available fungus that destroys a wide range of pest insects.

Beneficial insects – These good bugs, such as ladybugs and lacewings, can also be purchased and released. There is often a lag between the time a pest appears and when beneficial insects begin to control them, so be patient. A healthy and diverse garden with plenty of nectar sources will already be host to these beneficials. Knowing the life cycle of the pest is critical to determining when to release the predator.

Compost tea – Compost teas incorporate concentrated compost organisms to help control leaf and root diseases. They are sometimes effective and they won't harm beneficial organisms present in your garden. For more information on compost tea, turn to page 104.

Synthetic Pesticides

When all else fails, you may want to reach for a miracle cure—a handy spray bottle of some chemical that will eliminate your pest, weed, or disease problem. Just like those highly promoted ten-day miracle weight-loss diets, chemical pesticides—and their side effects—can be worse than the promised solutions.

Before you spray, consider the problem. Is it the result of a cultural condition that should be addressed, such as poor plant placement? Many poorly situated plants have succumbed to pest infestation—a cry for help from a plant that needs to be moved into the shade or out of wet soil.

Even if you spray, will the problem return? There are nontoxic choices. One may be as simple as removing the plant under attack and replacing it with a more resistant cultivar. A serious insect attack is often a clue that something is wrong with your garden environment. Ask yourself whether your soil is healthy, with plenty of organic matter. Check books or other references to be sure the afflicted plant is growing in the right place. Above all, be sure the plant is getting the right amount of light and water and not being overfertilized.

Guidelines for Chemical Use

- Don't use services that spray insecticides or herbicides on a prescheduled plan. You may end up overtreating the garden instead of making an informed decision based on regularly observing the needs of your landscape.

- If you have a service, be there when they spray so you can be sure you are getting what you're asking for.

- Ask nursery staff to help identify the least-toxic pesticide for your pest or disease problem. Order the *Grow Smart, Grow Safe* consumer guide to lawn and garden products. See the "Gardening Resources" section for information.

- Don't use broad-spectrum insecticides such as diazinon, chlorpyrifos (Dursban), Malathion, or carbaryl. These are likely to kill more of the natural enemies of pests.

- Avoid "weed and feed" and other pesticides that are broadcast over an entire yard. Instead, spot apply the least-toxic product only where you have a pest or weed.

- Buy only as much as you need. Unused pesticides are dangerous to store or dispose of. Empty pesticide containers should be placed in the garbage. Unused pesticides should be disposed of at your local hazardous waste disposal sites.

- Read and follow label directions carefully. Only use pesticides on the plants and pests listed on the product label. Apply exactly according to the directions.

- Be sure to wear specified protective clothing or equipment. Keep children and pets away from application areas for the specified time on the label or longer.

- Apply only when and where pests are present. There is no blanket solution to pesticide use. Address only a specific area or a specific pest of your garden.

▲ ▼ ▲ ▲ ▼ ▲ ▼ ▲ ▼ ▲ ▼ ▲ ▼ ▲ ▼

GOOD BUGS VERSUS BAD BUGS

As one of the Northwest's insect experts, Sharon Collman is buggy about all sorts of insects. And she readily shares her knowledge with other gardeners. As a longtime educator with the Washington State University Cooperative Extension and the Environmental Protection Agency, Collman helps home and commercial gardeners as well as farmers manage pests responsibly.

When I visited Collman, she held up a pint jar filled with hundreds of different bugs that she had collected in her backyard over a two-week period. "Even though I've studied my garden informally and observed plants and the beneficial and pest insects for years, I was blown away by the numbers of insects I'd never seen and the volume of beneficial or 'neutral' insects that were quietly going about their tasks," she notes. She explains that the good bugs are at the bottom of a complex food chain—a tasty meal for birds. If you spray to kill before informing yourself about their benign impact on ornamental garden plants, you become part of the problem. "In fact," says Collman, "only about 5 percent of all insects are 'pestiferous.' The other 95 percent play a vital role in a healthy garden and soil."

Most of the university research about invasive or troublesome pests is undertaken on behalf of an economically relevant cause—pests that can invade crops or forests. "Little is really known for backyards," Collman points out. "We've had to adapt the basic life cycle and biology research for home gardens and even nurseries. Until recently, there was little work on the biological control factors that might be at work." The majority of garden problems (as much as 75 percent, according to informal figures from the Washington State University/Puyallup Plant Clinic) are due to cultural and environmental influences. "*Not* bugs," Collman exclaims.

Collman advises that gardeners need to slow down and consider how to address nonbug problems first, before blaming the bugs. For example, when a lawn turns yellow, don't assume it's because of a crane fly infestation. Instead, first evaluate whether your lawn has poor drainage, has been compacted, or was insufficiently fertilized—all possible causes of yellow patches.

How Can We Outsmart Pests in Our Gardens?

"There are two types of invaders," Collman points out. Most of us consider any pest wreaking havoc in our gardens to be invasive (think about tent caterpillars, moths, flies, or root weevils). But a second, perhaps larger, problem is the exotic invader. These pests are new to the country, carried to our region, sometimes unwittingly, by humans. "Some of our most persistent garden pests are former exotic invaders that have established themselves here," Collman says.

She thinks that most backyard gardeners can happily coexist with pests. "It's actually pretty easy. Relax. By the time most people notice pests, beneficials are starting to find them too."

So often, when we spray insecticides we end up killing both the bad bugs and the beneficials. Collman warns, "That frequently allows surviving insects (and diseases) to rebound to higher levels. Good, healthy plants actually have a defense system and can mobilize chemicals or change their physical structure (such as thicker leaves or more surface hairs) to protect themselves if they are not over- or undercared for." You'll have a less susceptible garden when you pay attention to the health of the soil and grow plants where they're happiest. Remember, there's a human factor—*we* might be the baddest bugs around!

▲ ▼ ▲ ▲ ▼ ▲ ▼ ▲ ▼ ▲ ▼ ▲ ▼ ▲ ▼

▲ ▼ ▲ ▲ ▼ ▲ ▼ ▲ ▼ ▲ ▼ ▲ ▼ ▲ ▼

SUPPRESSING DISEASE WITH COMPOST TEA

Compost tea, a liquid extract of compost, is one of the hot new trends for gardeners, yet its origin dates back centuries to traditional farming practices. According to Ed Neff, a Seattle-based proponent of compost tea and cofounder of the Compost Tea Industry Association, this garden elixir had humble beginnings. "Liquid manure comes from farmers who for centuries made manure extracts. Farmers made early forms of compost tea by putting manures into gunnysacks and sticking them into big barrels of water; the sacks would sit there for a week and get good and stinky. Then they would pour the mixture on their plants—and it would promote growth and suppress diseases."

This age-old practice, Neff explains, had one limitation: it was anaerobic. Modern compost tea was born when agricultural researchers found that adding oxygen to a solution of water, nutrients, and microbes could help grow and incorporate beneficial organisms (including beneficial bacteria, fungi, protozoa, and nematodes). "Without air and without food, the microbes can't go anywhere, so companies started building equipment specifically designed to add oxygen to the water," he says. "They developed nutrients that are food for the microbes, such as composted manure or worm compost." Mix it all together in a nifty brewer and you've created a superconcentrated compost tea rich in microorganisms.

Compost tea fans say its application helps stimulate biological activity, improve soil structure, and enhance overall plant health and vigor. Reported benefits of using compost tea include enhanced disease suppression and reduced requirements for fungicide and fertilizer.

You can visit several Northwest specialty nurseries and buy a gallon or two of compost tea to take home. The trick is to use it within eight to twelve hours. Neff instructs,

"One gallon will cover 1,000 square feet. You can use it straight, by pouring onto roots, or you can use it as a foliar feed. Sprayed, sprinkled, or poured, the brew works best when applied in early morning or evening, after watering."

Steve Smith, past president of the Washington State Nursery and Landscape Association and owner of Sunnyside Nursery in Marysville, is another fan. "Using compost tea is just one tool to encourage microbial growth in the garden," he says. "In areas of the yard where it's not practical to incorporate organic matter, teas are a convenient way of reaping the benefits of compost without the hassle of toting wheelbarrows of the stuff through the yard."

Other believers point out that it can be applied to the leaves, twigs, bark, and soil—versus compost, which won't cling to foliage and thus can only be applied to the soil. Compost tea experts agree that it is important to use both; compost tea isn't a substitute for applying compost.

Many gardeners who consistently use compost tea praise its use, while others say they have not seen measurable results. What we do know is that compost tea is organic and won't damage you, the environment, or your pets. "There's no instant gratification," Neff concedes. "We do get reports from people who notice a difference, especially when they've had a garden or yard that's been under a lot of stress."

General maintenance practices are well suited for six to eight applications per year, according to another trade group, the International Compost Tea Council. Not surprisingly, compost tea's good effects are most noticeable in landscapes that have been disturbed due to the construction process or those that have been exposed to overuse of pesticides, leaving the garden "lifeless."

For more information on compost tea, check pages 123–124 in "Gardening Resources."

▲ ▼ ▲ ▲ ▼ ▲ ▼ ▲ ▼ ▲ ▼ ▲ ▼ ▲ ▼

Trouble-Free Plants

This list includes plants known to naturally resist Pacific Northwest diseases and pests. They are widely available through retail nurseries.

Evergreen Shrubs

Abelia grandiflora (abelia) – Delicate pink flowers bloom mid-summer to autumn; sun to part shade; bronzy red young leaves. Zones 6–9.

Cistus spp. (rock rose) – Gray or green foliage; quick growth; drought tolerant; poor soil; various flower colors with summer blooms. Zones 8–10.

Cotoneaster spp. (cotoneaster) – Early summer blooms, followed by persistent red berries; sun to part shade; nice informal hedge. Zones 5–8.

Lavandula angustifolia (lavender) – Fragrant lavender flowers, silvery foliage; very drought tolerant; sun; long flowering season from mid- to late summer. Zones 5–8.

Osmanthus delavayi (osmanthus) – Fragrant white flowers appear mid- to late spring; sun to shade; grows in poor soil. Zones 7–9.

Sarcococca spp. (sweet box) – Fragrant flowers in winter; shade. Zones 6–9.

Deciduous Shrubs

Caryopteris x *clandonensis* (bluebeard) – Extremely drought tolerant; deep-blue flowers late summer to early autumn; sun. Zones 6–9.

Cornus alba 'Elegantissima' (variegated red-twig dogwood) – Showy green and white foliage with red stems; late spring to early summer blooms; tolerates wet, clay soils; sun to shade. Zones 2–8.

Ribes sanguineum (red flowering currant) – Magenta spring flowers; edible blue berries; sun to shade. Zones 6–8.

Spiraea x *vanhouttei* or *S. thunbergii* (spirea) – White flowers in spring to early summer; sun to light shade. Zones 5–8.

Viburnum bodnantense 'Dawn' (Dawn viburnum) – Fragrant pink
flowers in late winter to early spring; striking foliage; sun to
part shade. Zones 7–8.

Evergreen Trees

Arbutus unedo (strawberry tree) – Reddish brown bark; white
flowers in autumn, followed by edible fruit; sun to part
shade; grows to ten feet. Zones 7–9.

Juniperus chinensis 'Torulosa' (Hollywood juniper) – Interesting
conifer form to twenty feet; produces cones in spring; sun.
Zones 3–9.

Prunus lusitanica (Portugal laurel) – Dark-green foliage on red
stems; dense hedge to twenty feet; fragrant white flowers in
early spring; sun to shade. Zones 7–9.

Deciduous Trees

Amelanchier x *grandiflora* 'Autumn Brilliance' (serviceberry) –
Showy spring flowers; fall color; edible fruit; open form to
twenty-five feet; sun to part shade. Zones 5–8.

Cercidiphyllum japonicum (katsura) – Colorful autumn color and
fragrance; sun to part shade (needs consistent water to
establish); to forty feet. Zones 4–8.

Liquidambar styraciflua (sweet gum) – Maple-like colorful fall
leaves; sun; to forty feet. 'Golden Treasure' is an attractive
choice, with variegated dark yellow and green foliage.
Zones 6–9.

Styrax japonicus (Japanese snowbell) – Hanging, fragrant white
flower clusters in early summer; graceful form to twenty
feet. Zones 6–8.

Roses

*Why grow finicky, disease-prone roses when there are some superb
varieties that resist black spot, powdery mildew, and rust? Plant
your roses where they get plenty of sun and good air circulation.
Give them rich soil, steady water, and a complete organic fertilizer
in spring for the best results.*

'Altissimo' – Deep red; climber; spring to fall blooms. Zones 5–9.

'Cécile Brunner' – Multiple pale-pink flowers, polyantha; spring to early autumn blooms. Zones 5–9.

'Climbing America' – Coral-orange; climber; spring to early autumn blooms. Zones 6–9.

'Europeana' – Dark red; floribunda; spring to early autumn blooms. Zones 4–9.

'Fantin-Latour' – Light pink-lavender; centifolia; early summer blooms. Zones 4–9.

'Fragrant Cloud' – Red-orange; stunning fragrance; hybrid tea; spring to autumn blooms. Zones 5–9.

'Just Joey' – Big, copper-pink summer to autumn blooms; hybrid tea. Zones 5–9.

'Pascali' – Double white flowers bloom spring to autumn; hybrid tea. Zones 5–9.

'Queen Elizabeth' – Large, deep-pink flowers; grandiflora; spring to autumn blooms. Zones 5–9.

Rhododendrons

These varieties are not prone to powdery mildew and are resistant to root weevil.

'Cilpinense' – Early apple-blossom–pink flowers in early spring, fading to white. Zones 8–9.

'Dora Amateis' – White flowers that nearly cover the plant in mid-spring. Zones 6–9.

'Oceanlake' – Medium-blue flowers in spring; low-growing form. Zones 6–9.

'PJM' – Small lavender flowers in early spring; small foliage on dwarf compact shrub. Zones 4–8.

'Rose Elf' – White to flushed violet–pink flowers bloom in early spring; dwarf variety with many blooms. Zones 4–8.

'Sapphire' – Blue spring flowers; small dense shrublet. Zones 4–8.

(Source: Local Hazardous Waste Management Program in King Co.)

Less Is More

From a design perspective, lawns are beautiful when they provide a restful, verdant counterpoint to exuberant borders. They can also give the kids a fun play area, protect soil from erosion, and filter out urban pollutants. But if lawn is one of the major features of your yard, it's probably time to reconsider the amount of turf you have. If you're like me, shrinking the lawn is an ongoing preoccupation. As my children are getting older, I've finally realized they don't need a football field– sized place to play. Each year, I enjoy carving out sections of the lawn's perimeter, taking on the design challenge of incorporating new plants I'm yearning to grow.

Less is more for many reasons, both aesthetic and environmental. You can diversify your garden and replace lawn with other material such as ground covers, ornamental berms, or paving material that drains well (crushed rock, paving stones, or cobbles). Not only will you be shrinking your lawn, but you'll shrink your water bill as well.

While you're beginning to scheme new ideas for ripping out grass and replacing it with a gorgeous mixed perennial-and-shrub border, you can start gardening more responsibly by changing your lawn care practices. Here are some methods to try.

Avoid overwatering. At a time when our water resources are at their lowest, more than 40 percent of our region's summer water use is devoted to watering lawns. The worst part is that the water you spray or sprinkle on the grass doesn't always reach its intended target. Runoff, evaporation, overspraying, and overwatering ensure that we're wasting water. Overwatering is also to blame for lawn disease. A one-inch "drink" of water per week is sufficient for most Northwest lawns. To avoid overwatering, conduct a "tuna can test" by placing several clean tuna cans around your lawn as receptacles. Turn on your sprinkler(s) for fifteen minutes, then stop and measure the water depth in each can. If the cans are filled to the top, you've proven that a once-weekly fifteen-minute session with the sprinkler is all your lawn needs. Adjust your watering times according to how much water collects in your tuna cans (for example, if the cans are one-quarter inch full, you'll need to water four-times as long, or one hour weekly).

Stop polluting with pesticides and fertilizers. Rainwater can carry pesticides and fertilizers from our lawns, through the groundwater, and into storm drains, where they end up polluting streams and lakes. Home gardeners overuse most common gardening pesticides, herbicides, and fertilizers. To avoid polluting, switch to using only environmentally safe pesticides, herbicides, or fungicides. Feed your lawn moderately, using an organic fertilizer.

Cut costs. To cut costs, consider letting your lawn go dormant during the hottest summer months. Replace sections of grass with drought-tolerant or low-water-use plantings or ground covers. Mow your lawn less frequently and try "grass-cycling." With increased amounts of cut grass overloading composting facilities during the warm season, the practice of leaving clippings on your lawn not only reduces demand on curbside yard waste programs, it makes for a great fertilizer for the soil and root system.

Tip

SMART MOWING: SAVE TIME, MONEY, AND ENERGY

- **Mow when the grass is dry.**
- **Set cutting height up to two to two and one-half inches.**
- **Remove only one-third of grass length. Cut a maximum of one inch each time you mow.**
- **If the grass is overgrown, mow twice—at a high setting, followed by a lower one.**
- **Mow every five to seven days in spring; twice a month in summer.**
- **Water and fertilize less.**
- **Recycle grass clippings as an organic fertilizer.**
- **Keep mower blades sharp by sharpening them twice a year.**

Good Garden Wishes

Live in Harmony

Though we may not always realize it, being a gardener is a transforming experience, one that gives each of us a healthy respect for nature—both that which is in our own backyards and the larger environment beyond. When we want our cherished garden to be free of toxic chemicals, infertile soil, or invasive plants, we eventually have to look over the fence to see the importance of having similar goals for the larger world around us. If you take one lesson from this book, I hope it's this: work with nature rather than fight against it.

It's easier (and uses fewer resources) to embrace and appreciate the contours of your land rather than renting a backhoe to remove trees, push around rocks, and dig up soil. It's more rewarding to integrate into the garden design a lineup of interesting native plants that you already know will thrive in this region than it is to pump up some high-maintenance varieties with too many fertilizers, the horticultural equivalent of steroids. It is far less stressful to change your idea of perfection in the garden—redefining *beauty* and thereby tolerating and accepting the presence of a few inevitable bugs and weeds. Instead of running around trying to make everything perfect, you can relax in a comfortable Adirondack chair and sip a cool beverage, gazing on the breathtaking beauty of a new bud about to

emerge or appreciating a stunning foliage composition
in a favorite container.

Finding Balance

I have a friend who is a talented gardener, one whose
beautiful, secluded landscape is envied and emulated by
many of those who've visited it. Now, later in life, he's
embraced technology, learning how to surf the Web for all
sorts of unique plant sources from around the globe, corre-
sponding with like-minded gardeners in far-flung places.
Rumor has it that my friend is so wired to the Internet that
he's spending more time at the keyboard than he is getting
his hands dirty in the garden.

Those of us who buy and read every new garden title
suffer some of the same bad habits. I confess to struggling
with reality at the other end of the spectrum. We have a joke
around my house that I tend to spend too much time "doing"
and not enough time "being."

In a search for balance, I know I should slow down and
"be" a little more. But I want to qualify my doing and being,
especially because when working in the garden, the two
are not mutually exclusive. My health (mental and physical)
improves when I'm in the garden. Weeding, planting, pruning,
and deadheading are activities that help me relax. Not all
these activities may be relaxing for you; spend the most
time doing the one(s) that you enjoy.

There's a synergy between being and doing in the
garden. Learn as you go. Yes, you can attend workshops,
read more books, go on garden tours, and check out
horticultural Web sites. But the most important piece of
advice I can give you is this: get into the garden and
discover what's there. You'll learn more about the unique
characteristics and qualities of your garden by digging in
it and getting your hands dirty.

Learning from Successes and Mistakes

There are far more discoveries and triumphs at your fingertips than there are potential disasters to worry about. One of my college friends often inspired me with her can-do attitude about life, especially when she would exclaim, "Oh, just put wheels on it!" In other words, get going, move forward, and enjoy the journey. Experiment in the garden and see what you learn.

Plants are so forgiving; they don't really require us to be experts in order to appreciate them while they grow. So often, they can do their thing quite well without much effort on our part.

I hope the ideas and resources included in these pages will help you to put wheels on your wheelbarrow. In writing the *Pacific Northwest Garden Survival Guide*, I've sought to unravel some of the explanations about the Pacific Northwest's unique gardening environment—the soil, the water (or lack of it), and the uninvited guests that arrive in the form of bugs, weeds, and diseases. As much as we might complain about tough soil or rainy winters and dry summers, we need to remember how truly fortunate we are to live in the Pacific Northwest. We can grow and enjoy more types of plants here than nearly anywhere else on earth. We can appreciate our gardens during every season of the year. And we have amazing resources at our fingertips to help us with the process.

I'm wowed and inspired by the talented horticultural veterans who've willingly shared their advice in these pages. They've recommended practical techniques to help demystify the universal frustrations faced by gardeners and provided "success tips" that you can try in your own backyard. I owe them many bouquets of thanks and appreciation for their generosity.

Like me, I hope you'll be blessed with the discovery that gardeners are indeed generous beings—and if you haven't learned this lesson yourself, go ahead and start the process. Lean over the gate and share your advice, swap ideas, or offer an extra plant or a handful of seeds to a curious beginner. You'll be nurturing the next garden survivor.

Gardening Resources

Display Gardens

There are so many wonderful public and private gardens to inspire Pacific Northwest gardeners that you'll need a few years to see them all. Those listed here represent only a small selection. Many of these gardens—and countless others worth visiting—are featured in *The Northwest Gardeners' Resource Directory*, ninth edition, for which I served as editor (Sasquatch Books, 2002).

OREGON

Berry Botanic Garden

> 11505 SW Summerville Avenue, Portland, OR 97219
> (503) 636-4112   www.berrybot.org
> *The 6.5-acre garden is noteworthy for its display of Northwest native plants, specimen trees and shrubs, and perennials. The garden has a respected conservation program where you can learn about endangered native plants of our region.*

Clackamas Community College
John Inskeep Environmental Learning Center

> 19600 S. Molalla Avenue, Oregon City, OR 97045
> (503) 657-6958 ext. 2351 (weekdays)
> http://depts.clackamas.edu/elc/index.asp
> *A five-acre nature education center featuring a composting demonstration site, environmentally friendly garden displays, a wetlands restoration site, and wildlife gardens.*

Hoyt Arboretum

4000 SW Fairview Boulevard, Portland, OR 97221

(503) 228-8733   www.hoytarboretum.org

Portland's urban forest is 175 acres large, with ten miles of hiking trails. With 950 species of trees and shrubs, this is a fabulous destination for exploring a world of woody plants.

Metro's Demonstration Garden

6800 SE 57th Avenue (at Cooper Street), Portland, OR

(503) 234-3000   www.metro-region.org

Designed to replicate a typical Portland residential lot (116 feet by 50 feet), the garden helps visitors learn about the benefits of using natural gardening techniques to grow healthy plants while protecting the quality of our rivers, streams, and wildlife habitat.

Mount Pisgah Arboretum

33735 Seavy Loop Road, Eugene, OR 97405

(541) 747-3817   www.efn.org/~mtpisgah

Mount Pisgah Arboretum covers more than 200 acres of diverse ecological habitats, including forested hillsides, waterways, and a riparian meadow.

The Oregon Garden

879 W. Main Street, Silverton, OR 97381

(503) 874-8100   www.oregongarden.org

Using a landscape approach for displaying plants, the garden is both attractive and educational. Among the many appealing display gardens are those featuring water plantings, edibles, conifers, roses, Northwest-style plantings, and bird habitats.

WASHINGTON

Bellevue Botanical Garden

12001 Main Street, Bellevue, WA 98005

(425) 452-2750   www.bellevuebotanical.org

Features the Water-Wise Demonstration Garden with a diverse selection of plants that thrive in the Northwest. The project was created by designers Jil and Howard Stenn (see my interview with Howard Stenn on pages 34–35).

Center for Urban Horticulture/Orin and Althea Soest
Herbaceous Display Garden

3501 NE 41st Street, Seattle, WA 98195

(206) 543-8616   www.urbanhort.org

This idea garden features eight pie-shaped display beds providing gardeners with examples of nearly 300 different herbaceous plants grown in a variety of typical backyard conditions.

Evergreen Arboretum and Gardens

Legion Memorial Park

145 Alverson Boulevard (at West Marine View Drive)

Everett, WA 98201

(425) 257-8300   www.evergreenarboretum.com

When you visit Evergreen Arboretum, take note of the water conservation garden and the entry garden that demonstrates the best choices for urban street trees.

The Kruckeberg Botanic Garden

20066 15th Avenue NW, Shoreline, WA 98177

(206) 542-4777   www.kruckeberg.org

Here is an inspiring garden, not only because it showcases a mind-boggling array of plants thriving within a four-acre site, but also because it represents the life work of Arthur Kruckeberg, author of Gardening with Native Plants of the Pacific Northwest, *and his late wife, Mareen Kruckeberg.*

Lakehaven Conservation Demonstration Garden

French Lake Park, 31531 First Avenue South

Federal Way, WA 98063

(253) 946-5426   www.lakehaven.org/conservation.htm

This educational garden, created by the Lakehaven Utility District, helps visitors learn how to reduce the amount of water applied to the landscape.

Point Defiance Park

5400 N. Pearl Street, Tacoma, WA 98405

(253) 305-1000   www.tacomaparks.com

Along with its world-renowned zoo, Point Defiance Park is home to numerous display gardens, from a coastal forest to a moist woodland to the arid pine forest of the Eastern Cascades.

Seattle Tilth Gardens

4649 Sunnyside Avenue North, Room One

Seattle, WA 98103

(206) 633-0451   www.seattletilth.org

A visit to Seattle Tilth will introduce you to edible gardening practices, great composting ideas (a Master Composter program is housed here), a solar greenhouse, and a well-labeled weed bed.

Washington State University/King County Master Gardener Urban Demonstration Garden

15680 SE 16th Street, Bellevue, WA 98007

(425) 644-9601   www.metrokc.gov/wsu-ce

This working demonstration garden is open year-round, and you'll meet knowledgeable Master Gardener volunteers here from April through October.

Organizations to Contact

Here are some useful organizations; all are great resources for answering your "garden survival" questions.

Native Plant Society of Oregon

P.O. Box 902, Eugene, OR 97440

(503) 248-9242   www.npsoregon.org

With thirteen chapters throughout the state and more than 1,000 members, the Native Plant Society of Oregon is dedicated to the state's native vegetation. A membership will give you access to a local chapter of enthusiasts, a newsletter subscription, field trips, and workshops.

Noxious Weed Control Program, Oregon Department of Agriculture

635 Capitol Street NE, Salem, OR 97301-2532

503) 986-4550

www.oda.state.or.us/Plant/weed_control/index.html

Oregon's noxious weed-control program seeks to protect the state's natural resources from the invasion and proliferation of exotic noxious weeds.

Oregon Master Gardeners

OSU Extension Horticulture Department
Oregon State University, 4017 Ag & Life Science Building
Corvallis, OR 97331-7304
(541) 737-3464   http://osu.orst.edu/extension/mg/
This site will link you to the OSU online plant disease control and pest management guidelines sites, as well as contacts for Master Gardening programs in more than twenty counties.

PlantAmnesty

P.O. Box 15377, Seattle, WA 98115
(206) 783-9813   www.plantamnesty.org
The organization's mission is to "end the senseless torture and mutilation of trees and shrubs caused by malpruning." You can gain a fabulous education by joining PlantAmnesty, attending a workshop, or checking its list of recommended landscapers and arborists.

Washington Master Gardeners

7612 Pioneer Way East, WSU Puyallup Research and
Extension Center, Puyallup, WA, 98371-4998
(877) 978-6448   http://mastergardener.wsu.edu
This comprehensive Washington State University Extension site will link you to county Master Gardener offices statewide.

Washington Native Plant Society

7400 Sand Point Way NE, Seattle, WA 98115
(206) 527-3210   www.wnps.org
Membership in the society will connect you with other like-minded plant-lovers who are dedicated to the preservation, conservation, and study of Washington's native plants.

Washington State Noxious Weed Board

Natural Resources Building
1111 Washington Street SE, Olympia, WA, 98504
Mail: P.O. Box 42560, Olympia, WA 98504-2560
(360) 902-1901   www.nwcb.wa.gov
Here's where Washington residents can start their education about weeds and programs to eradicate them.

Hotlines

Plant Answer Line

(206) UW-PLANT (206-897-5268)

This hotline is operated through the Elisabeth C. Miller Horticultural Library at University of Washington's Center for Urban Horticulture.

Washington State University Community Library

(206) 296-DIAL (206-296-3425) or

(800) 325-6165 ext. 63425 (outside King County)

Gardeners can access more than 250 informative recorded messages that address a wide array of questions about everything from lawns to roses and more.

Web Sites and Publications

Great Plant Picks

The Elisabeth C. Miller Botanical Garden

www.greatplantpicks.org

A regional plant awards program to help the home gardener identify unbeatable plants for Pacific Northwest gardens, ach year announcing its choices of superb plants.

Grow Smart, Grow Safe: A Consumer Guide to Lawn and Garden Products

By Philip Dickey, Washington Toxics Coalition

Produced by the Local Hazardous Waste Management Program in King County. Order from Washington Toxics Coalition, (206) 632-1545 ext. 7   www.watoxics.org

Grow Smart, Grow Safe is a user-friendly booklet that rates 450 brand-name pest control products for health and environmental hazards. Fertilizers and soil amendments are also listed.

Local Hazardous Waste Management Program in King County: Trouble-Free Plants for the Pacific Northwest

www.metrokc.gov/hazwaste/house/plantlist.html

Here is a site offering useful lists of plants that resist diseases and pests naturally, thereby reducing your need to use pesticides and other damaging chemicals.

Metro Recycling

www.metro-region.org/gardening

> *Portland's Metro Recycling operates a fabulous Natural Gardening and Composting program. This Web site offers information about composting, lawn care, pest and weed control, and tips on choosing plants that will resist pests and disease.*

Oregon State University Extension and Experiment Station Communications

http://eesc.orst.edu

> *This extensive and user-friendly site is your ticket to hundreds of articles on Northwest gardening topics from fruit growing to native habitats.*

The Pacific Northwest Gardener's Book of Lists

(Taylor Publishing Co., 208 pages, 1997)

> *Every Northwest gardener should have Ray and Jan McNeilan's excellent plant reference on their shelves. This book offers more than 200 lists of proven plants for any growing condition.*

Seattle Public Utilities

(206) 684-SAVE (206-684-7283) www.savingwater.org

> *Funded by a coalition of Puget Sound–area cities and water/sewer districts, the Saving Water Partnership has produced a wonderful series of publications, available upon request via the Web site or by phone.*

Stop Before You Spray—Good Bugs Guide

www.metrokc.gov/hazwaste/house/garden/goodbugs.html

> *Check out this great online guide and photographic source that will help you identify "good bugs." You can order a printed version of this useful tool from Seattle Audubon Nature Bookshop, 8050 35th Ave. NE, Seattle, WA 98115. Send $3.95 each plus $2 handling (Washington state residents need to also add 8.8 percent sales tax). Call (206) 523-4483 or e-mail goodbugsguide@seattleaudubon.org.*

Supplies, Equipment, and Materials

Composts, Mulches, and Soils

Bailey Compost

12711 Springhetti Road, Snohomish, WA 98296

(360) 568-8826

A custom mix of 90 percent compost and 10 percent dairy manure.

Cedar Grove Composting Inc.

17825 Cedar Grove Road SE, Maple Valley, WA 98038

(800) 764-SOILS-4U (800-764-5748)

www.cedar-grove.com

Cedar Grove transforms grass, leaves, yard trimmings, food waste, and wood waste into nutrient-rich compost.

Earth-Wise Compost

Metro Regional Solid Waste and Recycling

600 NE Grand Avenue, Portland, OR 97232

(503) 234-3000

Earth-Wise works with private composting companies to test and certify yard waste products. Contact them for a current listing of certified compost suppliers in your neighborhood.

GroCo

Distributed by Sawdust Supply, 15 S. Spokane Street

Seattle, WA 98134

(206) 622-5141   www.sawdustsupply.com

Use GroCo, a naturally composted mixture of three parts sawdust to one part biosolids, as compost for sandy or clay soil.

Pacific Topsoils Inc.

(800) 884-SOIL (800-884-7645)

www.pacifictopsoils.com

Pacific Topsoils offers a great selection of mulches, bark, topsoil, and specialty mixes.

TAGRO

City of Tacoma, Public Works Department

Environmental Services/Wastewater Management

2201 Portland Avenue, Tacoma, WA 98421

(253) 502-2150   www.ci.tacoma.wa.us/tagro

TAGRO Mix is a nutrient-rich soil conditioner made from biosolids, an organic by-product of Tacoma's treated wastewater, blended with sand and sawdust.

Whitney Farms

P.O. Box 70, Independence, OR 97351

(800) 531-4411   www.whitneyfarms.com

A leading producer of potting soils, soil amendments, and organic fertilizers for western gardeners.

Non–Toxic Garden Products

Gardens Alive

5100 Schenley Place, Lawrenceburg, IN 47025

(513) 354-1482   www.gardensalive.com

This cool mail order catalog features hundreds of environmentally responsible gardening products and supplies.

Safer Brand Insecticide Killing Soap

(800) 800-1819   www.victorpest.com

Safer Brand Insecticide Killing Soap kills pests such as aphids, mealy bugs, and whiteflies without harming beneficial insects.

Weed Prevention Plus

(800) 800-1819   www.victorpest.com

Weed Prevention Plus is a 100-percent corn gluten pre-emergent herbicide. The chemical-free product inhibits the germination of various common weeds.

Compost Tea Organizations

Compost Tea Industry Association

P.O. Box 71894, Eugene, OR 97401

(541) 345-2855 www.composttea.org

International Compost Tea Council
> 14150 NE 20th Street, Suite 293, Bellevue, WA 98007
> (425) 558-0990 or (866) 558-0990   www.intlctc.org

Drip Irrigation

Dripworks
> 190 Sanhedrin Circle, Willits, CA 95490
> (800) 522-3747   www.dripworksusa.com

The Urban Farmer
> 2833 Vicente Street, San Francisco, CA 94114
> (415) 661-2204 or (800) 753-3747
> www.urbanfarmerstore.com

DIG
> 1210 Activity Drive, Vista, CA 92083
> (800) 344-2281   www.digcorp.com

Eco-Turf-Grass Seed

Hobbes and Hopkins
> 1712 SE Akeny Street, Portland, OR 97214
> (503) 239-7518   www.protimelawnseed.com

Soil Amendments

Starbucks' Grounds for your Garden Program
> www.starbucks.com/aboutus/compost.asp
> *This grassroots effort supplies used coffee grounds to gardeners through their local Starbucks store. Coffee grounds can be applied directly to the acid-loving plants in your garden or added to home compost and worm bins.*

The Oregon Zoo's Elephant Zoo Doo
Best Buy Landscape Supplies
21600 NW Amberwood Drive, Hillsboro, OR 97124
(503) 645-6665 or (503) 645-2275
The world's most prolific herd of captive Asian elephants as well as other herbivores manufactures this ZooDoo for your garden. Limited availability; call for details.

Woodland Park Zoo Doo
601 N. 59th Street, Seattle, WA 98103
(206) 625-POOP   www.zoo.org
Twice each year, Seattle's Woodland Park Zoo offers its Zoo Doo to area gardeners. Call the hotline to find out dates of the next Zoo Doo sale.

Gravel/Stone

Manufacturer's Minerals
1215 Monster Road SW, Renton, WA 98055
(425) 228-2120

Soil-Testing Resources

In addition to contacting these commercial soil-testing and analysis firms, you can contact your Master Gardener office for local soil-testing recommendations.

EarthCo, Inc.
P.O. Box 50084, Street, Saint Louis, MO 63105
(314) 994-2167   www.earthtest.com

Peaceful Valley Farm Supply
P.O. Box 2209, Grass Valley, CA 95945
(530) 272-4769   www.groworganic.com

Ribeiro Plant Lab Inc.
10744 NE Manitou Beach Drive
Bainbridge Island, WA 98110
(206) 842-1157   www.ribeiroplantlab.com

Experts

I've interviewed or quoted the following individuals throughout the *Pacific Northwest Garden Survival Guide*. I'm thankful for their sage advice! If you are interested in learning more about these wise folks, their companies, or projects, read on.

AccuWeather.com

When you visit www.accuweather.com, a fantastic Web site for local, national and international weather information, check the "Gardening" section for garden-friendly weather news. Here you can enter your zip code and read a gardening forecast for your own neighborhood. Precipitation maps and planning maps are also worth noting.

Van Bobbitt, instructor and arboretum coordinator
South Seattle Community College
Landscape Horticulture Program
6000 16th Avenue SW, Seattle, WA 98106
(206) 768-6717   www.sccd.ctc.edu/south

Sharon Collman
US EPA, Region 10
Community Involvement Unit ECO-081
1200 Sixth Avenue
Seattle, WA 98101
(206) 553-0038   collmans@wsu.edu

Carolyn Devine, education director
Berry Botanic Garden
1505 SW Summerville Avenue
Portland, OR 97219
(503) 636-4112   www.berrybot.org

Tory Galloway

Piriformis Nursery

1031 N. 35th Street, Seattle, WA 98103

(206) 632-1760   www.piriformis.com

Dan Hinkley

Heronswood Nursery

7530 NE 288th Street, Kingston, WA 98346

(360) 297-4172   www.heronswood.com

The extensive online Heronswood Nursery catalog features more than 2,000 fabulous plants. Order your own copy for $5.

Sean Hogan

Cistus Nursery

22711 NW Gillihan Road, Portland, OR 97231

(503) 621-2233   www.cistus.com

Maurice Horn

Joy Creek Nursery

20300 NW Watson Road, Scappoose, OR 97056

(503) 543-7474   www.joycreek.com

Susan McCoy, president

Garden Media Group

P.O. Box 758, Chadds Ford, PA 19317

(610) 388-9330   www.gardenmediagroup.com

Visit the Web site to read Garden Media Group's "What's In-What's Out" annual garden industry forecast.

Philip Mote, Ph.D.

University of Washington

P.O. Box 354235, Seattle, WA 98195

(206) 616-5346

Visit the Web site of the Washington State climatologist at www.climate.washington.edu.

The site includes links to sources of climate data and seasonal forecasts for the state of Washington. Most data on the site are available for free.

Ed Neff, co-founder and president

Soil Soup Inc.

305 Ninth Avenue North, Seattle, WA 98109

(206) 405-4385   www.soilsoup.com

Mary Robson

marysophia@earthlink.net.

*You can read Mary's columns on the "Practical Gardener"
page each Wednesday in the* Seattle Times *at
www.seattletimes.com. Mary has enjoyed twenty years
of experience speaking to gardeners in the Pacific Northwest
and enjoys meeting with groups of all sizes and types.*

Steve Smith

Sunnyside Nursery

3915 Sunnyside Boulevard, Marysville, WA 98271

(425) 334-2002   sunnysidenursery@msn.com

Howard and Jil Stenn

Stenn Design

21716 Westside Highway SW

Vashon Island, WA 98070

(260) 463-6523   bedigger@aol.com

*Specializing in landscape design, resource conservation,
and education*

Acknowledgments

The first person to thank is Marlene Blessing, the former editor-in-chief at Fulcrum Publishing who came to me with the idea of developing a "Garden Survival" handbook. She described this project to me as a "little book with useful information, friendly and no-nonsense … kind of like a supertips guide." If the words I've written land anywhere close to this description, I feel lucky to have followed Marlene's original vision!

A savvy and talented editor and book creator, Marlene had the insight and understanding of issues facing gardeners in the Pacific Northwest and other regions—and she devised a creative format for communicating them in a handy user-friendly book. Writing about our precious resources—soil, water, and the environment—may not be as sexy as writing about garden design, but it is essential to our success as gardeners.

I'm equally grateful for the horticultural editing, support, and enthusiasm of the series editor, Cathy Wilkinson Barash. She stepped up to the plate and shepherded this slim volume through to its final format in a less-than-ideal time frame. I love Cathy's practical approach to editing and her sense of humor— I'm lucky she came aboard at the right time to help me finish the manuscript. Likewise, Fulcrum editor Faith Marcovecchio defied ridiculous deadlines to put the finishing touches on the text. Faith also brought a calm sense of order to my work, and I am so appreciative.

The brilliant and talented experts interviewed for and featured in the Pacific Northwest Garden Survival Guide sidebars have been integral to creating this book's spirit and personality. Each has shared valuable ideas, observations, and advice. Thank you to Mary Robson ("Practical Gardener" columnist for the Seattle Times and former Washington State University Extension agent for King and Snohomish Counties); Howard Stenn (Stenn Design, Vashon Island, Washington); Maurice Horn (Joycreek Nursery, Scappoose, Oregon); Dr. Philip Mote (Washington state climatologist and University of Washington research scientist); Tory Galloway (Piriformis Nursery, Seattle); Carolyn Devine (education director

for the Berry Botanic Garden, Portland); Van Bobbitt (Landscape
Horticulture Department, South Seattle Community College);
Sharon Collman (Environmental Protection Agency and
Washington State University/Cooperative Extension); Ed Neff
(Compost Tea Industry Association and Soil Soup); Steve Smith
(Washington State Nursery and Landscape Association and
Sunnyside Nursery, Marysville, Washington); and Bernard Rayno,
a forecaster with AccuWeather.com.

A special thanks to Liz Fikejs, David McDonald, Carl
Woestwin, and Nota Lucas of Seattle Public Utilities and the
Saving Water Partnership for their enthusiasm and assistance in
allowing me to excerpt portions of the Natural Lawn and Garden
series. My pal Mary Raybourn of King County Department of
Natural Resources generously shared the county's fabulous Stop
Before You Spray—Good Bugs brochure for use in the book.

Finally, I owe love and gratitude to Bruce, Benjamin, and
Alexander Brooks, my husband and sons, for their support and
faith in me. I dig you guys!

Index

Thirst-Aid and First-Aid Kit
for the Gardener's Bookshelf

**XERISCAPE
HANDBOOK**

A How-To Guide
to Natural Resource-
Wise Gardening

by Gayle Weinstein

ISBN 1-55591-346-6
$24.95 PB

**XERISCAPE
PLANT GUIDE**

100 Water-Wise
Plants for Gardens
and Landscapes

by Denver Water
Board

ISBN 1-55591-253-2
$27.95 PB

**XERISCAPE
COLOR GUIDE**

100 Water-Wise Plants
for Gardens and
Landscapes

by David Winger

ISBN 1-55591-391-1
$15.95 PB

**THE ZEN
OF GARDENING IN
THE HIGH
AND ARID WEST**

Tips, Tools, and
Techniques

by David Wann

ISBN 1-55591-457-8
$17.95 PB

**PESTS OF
THE WEST**

Prevention and
Control for
Today's Garden
and Small Farm

by Whitney
Cranshaw

ISBN 1-55591-401-2
$19.95 PB

**NATIVE PLANTS
FOR
HIGH-ELEVATION
WESTERN
GARDENS**

by Janice Busco and
Nancy R. Morin

ISBN 1-55591-475-6
$29.95 PB

FULCRUM PUBLISHING
16100 Table Mountain Parkway, Suite 300, Golden, CO, 80403
To order call 800-992-2908 or visit www.fulcrum-gardening.com
Also available at your local bookstore or gardening center